BACH'S
Well-Tempered Clavier

BACH'S
Well-Tempered Clavier

An Exploration of the
48 Preludes and Fugues

MARJORIE WORNELL ENGELS

McFarland & Company, Inc., Publishers
Jefferson, North Carolina, and London

LIBRARY OF CONGRESS CATALOGUING-IN-PUBLICATION DATA

Engels, Marjorie Wornell.
    Bach's well-tempered clavier : an exploration of the 48 preludes
and fugues / Marjorie Wornell Engels.
      p.   cm.
    Includes bibliographical references and index.

    ISBN-13: 978-0-7864-2544-0
    (softcover : 50# alkaline paper) ∞

    1. Bach, Johann Sebastian, 1685–1750. Wohltemperierte Klavier,
1. T.   2. Bach, Johann Sebastian, 1685–1750. Wohltemperierte
Klavier, 2. T.   3. Canons, fugues, etc. (Harpsichord)—Analysis,
appreciation.   4. Tonality.   I. Title.
MT145.B14E63 2006
786'.1872—dc22   2006003235

British Library cataloguing data are available

Cover art ©2006 Pictures Now

Manufactured in the United States of America

McFarland & Company, Inc., Publishers
  Box 611, Jefferson, North Carolina 28640
   www.mcfarlandpub.com

Dedicated to all who love the
Well-Tempered Clavier

Acknowledgments

I am deeply grateful to many friends and colleagues who assisted me during the many years this book was in preparation: the North Island Branch of the British Columbia Registered Music Teachers Association, who in the early years of my research, invited me to give five lectures on parts of the WTC, and whose enthusiastic response was pivotal to my decision to continue my work and present it as a book; Gwyneth Hoyle, John Burke, Helen Moats, and Ann Southam, who read some draft chapters, caught ambiguities, and always made perceptive suggestions for improvement; Marianela Cárcamo-Harley, who taped for me dozens of BBC programs on Bach; Elaine Broughton, J Havelaar, and Enid Havelaar who provided vital information; my dear brother, Lloyd Wornell, for his generosity, sound advice, and unbounded enthusiasm; Sandy and Justus Havelaar, who not only provided me with a word processor but continuously offered assistance and support in innumerable ways; Hubert Engels, who read the drafts of every chapter, caught the weak spots, suggested excellent changes, and, above all, encouraged me every step of the way; Melanie Reaveley and Lorelee Parker at our local branch of the Vancouver Island Regional Library, who so graciously and expertly tracked down and obtained books for my research from libraries across Canada and the United States. Without their help the project would have been impossible.

To all, my heartfelt thanks and gratitude.

Last, and most important, I am deeply indebted to the great Bach scholars, past and present, who inspired me and led the way.

Contents

Preface

In 1722 Bach completed the first book of 24 Preludes and Fugues in all the major and minor keys, which he titled *The Well-Tempered Clavier*, referring to the development of a keyboard tuning system that made it possible to modulate to several keys within a piece, and to extend the range to include keys of five, six, and seven sharps and flats. In his later years he began to compile a second set, which he completed in 1744.

This book is a study of Bach's musical language in *The Well-Tempered Clavier*, and explores in depth the emotional dimension he creates in each piece through harmonic design and melodic and rhythmic motivic formulas in accordance with the Baroque doctrine of affects, which stipulates that one mood govern one piece.

This exploration includes the significance of the tonality of each key, symbolism of melodic and rhythmic motifs and of numbers, and thematic and rhythmic links between a Prelude and it companion Fugue in each book, and between the pair in Book I and those in the same key in Book II. Reference is made to other instrumental works by Bach in the same key, and to choral works that contain revealing clues to the meaning of motifs, rhythmic and melodic patterns, and the relationship between key tonality and affect.

There are 24 chapters in the book, one for each of the major and minor keys, beginning with C major and proceeding chromatically through to B minor. A brief preamble to each key may include historical facts and mention relevant instrumental and choral compositions. This is followed by a detailed study of the four pieces in the key, each dealt with separately for easy reference.

The book is intended as a companion that introduces new aspects for contemplation, which will enrich teaching, playing, and listening, and lead to a more intimate communion with the music in *The Well-Tempered Clavier*.

Introduction

There is a wonderful anecdote about *The Well-Tempered Clavier* that is well worth repeating. One of Bach's students, Heinrich Nicolaus Gerber, told his son that on three occasions, Bach, "under the pretext of not feeling in the mood to teach," played through the entire first book for him. He counted these "among his happiest hours." We can only attempt to imagine and grasp such an experience. What would certainly be apparent was the love and personal attachment of the composer for this particular work among his creations. This remained throughout the rest of his life. He kept returning to it, revising details, and referring to it during his work on the second volume. As will be revealed and contemplated in my book, there are deeper implications. *The Well-Tempered Clavier* (*WTC*) may indeed be the most intimate of Bach's gifts to us.

The primary focus of this study of the *WTC* is on the musical language which, as Forkel tells us, Bach felt the composer as poet "must never be without sufficient expressions to represent his feelings" (in David and Mendel, *The Bach Reader*, p. 318).

The guiding principle of a composer at that time was the theory, or doctrine, of affects, that is, that one piece be governed by one emotion or mood. This was not new. Monteverdi, in the sixteenth century, had declared that "music should express the full range of human passions, from tranquility to anger, from joy to despair." It was, however, Geneva-born Jesuit antiquarian Athanasius Kircher (1602–80) who was the first to define the Baroque doctrine. Bach faithfully adhered to it, using rhythmic, melodic, and motivic formulas long established, or of his own device, to express a range of affects. Musical theorist Marpurg even drew up a list of 69 affects.

Very important in defining the mood and choosing the character of the language for a composition was the key tonality. Bach associated each tonality with a distinct emotional dimension. In the common keys, those up to four sharps and flats, each tonal association is most clearly defined in the choral works. Bach generally retained this dimension in the Preludes and Fugues in those keys in the WTC, then created singular, heightened dimensions for the "new" keys made possible by mean-temperament tuning. (Equal-temperament came later.)

Now we come to the language. In this realm we gain further insight into the astonishing scope of Bach's creative genius. It is also where Bach reveals himself on a most intimate level.

Symbolism in art and religion began with the dawn of civilization and continued to evolve through successive cultures. Bach knew all the forms of symbolism in music, which had been developing since as far back as the Middle Ages, and was acutely aware of their subliminal effect on the listener. He made it a vital part of his creative process.

One form he used can be described as pictorial symbolism. This he created through harmonic progression, certain melodic intervals, and melodic and rhythmic motifs and patterns. In the choral works, these may represent nature, such as the lightning and thunder chorus in the St. Matthew Passion, the flowing waters of rivers, waves of the ocean or lakes, the motion of clouds, according to the text in cantatas. Many depict emotional states of joy, happiness, weariness, sorrow, grief, anger, terror, again fitting a particular text.

Another form was numerical symbolism. The mystical and sacred meaning of numbers stems from ancient times, especially in the philosophy and teachings of Pythagoras. It is found throughout the biblical texts of the Old and New Testaments.

Bach was fascinated by numbers. He wove them into his music secretly, and often in astounding ways. They are revealed visually rather then aurally, but always contribute to an aural effect. Two of his special secret codes were the numbers 14 and 41, which represented Bach and J. S. Bach, respectively. How and where he encoded his name affects the essence of a particular passage or even a whole piece. Other instances of numerical symbolism are spectacular. The word credo is symbolized by the number 43. In the Credo of the B minor Mass, the word appears 43 times. In the St. Matthew Passion, when Jesus refuses to answer accusations of false witness, the tenor arioso, "My Jesus answers not," is accompanied by 39 chords, referring to Psalm 39, "I was dumb, I opened not my mouth." In the depiction of Jesus at the Last Supper, the bass recitative, "Drink ye all of it," consists of 116 notes, referring to Psalm 116, which is the only one mentioning the "Cup of Salvation."

The Preludes and Fugues abound in both these forms of symbolism.

The affect Bach expresses through each tonality has its own symbolic language of harmonic design, melodic and rhythmic motifs and patterns. In many cases he ingeniously carries forward certain of these, not only from a Prelude to its companion Fugue in Book I, but even to those in the same key in Book II. Although they often go through a process of transfiguration, their essential meaning remains the same.

The *WTC* is a very private work. From the title Bach gave to the first book, we know that he intended it for study and personal enjoyment. It was not meant for public performance. While we now can enjoy many opportunities to hear it performed by professional artists, it is by studying the score and playing the Preludes and Fugues ourselves that our appreciation increases exponentially, and the music affects us most deeply.

Many have read Casals's moving account of starting each day, for 80 years, by playing two of Bach's Preludes and Fugues on the piano. How it filled him with "awareness of the wonder of life, with a feeling of the incredible marvel of being a human being" (*Joys and Sorrows, Reflections of Pablo Casals as Told to Albert Kahn*, p. 17). But it is not only musicians for whom playing Bach is a vital part of life. Here is the great English actress Dame Sybil Thorndike during an interview: "I play a bit of Bach every day when I'm home ... when I wash up the breakfast things, I go and do half an hour of Bach. It does something for me mathematically. Its precision. Its wonderful construction. Its solidity. I think Bach is the nearest approach to God Almighty I've ever met on this earth" (Studs Terkel, *The Spectator*, p. 213).

The *WTC* is a monumental creation in the history of music. Marvel at Bach's supreme mastery of the craft of his art. Delight in the technical challenges he poses. But above all, listen to the great man himself speaking from the depth of his soul.

He considered music entirely as a language,
and the composer as a poet, who,
in whatever language he may write,
must never be without sufficient
expressions to represent his feelings.

—Forkel

1

C Major

C major, sometimes thought of as neutral, in Bach's hands became a vehicle for profound musical expression. He endowed it with strength, joy, confidence, spiritual energy and, above all, jubilant outpouring of praise and affirmation.

An abundance of music in C major flowed from his pen: the Preludes and Fugues in the *WTC*; an Invention; a Sinfonia; two pieces in the *Twelve Little Preludes* and one in the *Six Little Preludes*; concertos for two and three harpsichords; two organ concertos; three organ Preludes and Fugues (including the "Great"); an organ Trio Sonata; an organ Toccata; a Sonata for unaccompanied violin; a Suite for unaccompanied cello; and the first of the Orchestral Suites (Overtures).

Some of the most glorious choruses and arias in the Cantatas are in C major: the opening chorus of Cantata 172 *Erschallet ihr Lieder* (Resound, ye songs); the opening chorus of Cantata 147 *Herz und Mund und Tat und Leben* (Heart and voice and thought and action); the opening chorus of Cantata 70 *Wachet! betet, betet! Wachet!* (Watch ye, pray ye, watch ye); *Lobet den Herrn, alle Heiden* (Praise the Lord, all ye heathen) from Motet BWV 230; the bass aria in Cantata 172 *Heiligste Dreieinigkeit, grosser Gott der Ehren* (Holiest Trinity, great God of Glory); and the bass aria *Ich will von Jesu Wunder singen* (I will sing of the wonder of Jesus) in Cantata 147, with its brilliant trumpet parts.

I list these vocal works because if it is possible for you to listen to any of these, there is no greater way to enter into the spirit of this key as a preface to the study of its Preludes and Fugues.

Prelude, C Major, Book I

This first piece of one of the greatest works in the history of music enthralls us with the beauty and naturalness of its style and harmonic progression. Unembellished, pure in conception, a jewel in design, it speaks to the heart immediately.

It begins on the tonic note, a plan Bach carries through all the Preludes of Book I. While the broken chord is very familiar to us today, in fact it was historically an important development in music. The way they were broken became an art, enriching harmonic possibilities, challenging the performer with new technical demands and creating a gold mine for a composer's imagination.

The study of the broken chord becomes the focal point in this Prelude and in the C major pieces of the *Twelve* and *Six Little Preludes*. Bach, a master of this form, presents a variety of realizations—tied-over notes, passing between the hands, accompanying a solid form.

Shining through all these technical devices is, of course, the music, full of grace and inner joy, movingly captured in this opening to the *WTC*.

Fugue, C Major, Book I

Using the rising scale, Bach strides forth with the confidence of a supremely skilled master, which he will abundantly display throughout this Fugue. This affirmation of the tonic key becomes a signature phrase for many pieces in C major.

In this imposing subject melody Bach ingeniously makes a direct link with its companion Prelude. The first seven top notes of the chords of the Prelude appear in the same order within the first section of the theme of the Fugue.

Number symbolism was very much a part of Bach's musical language; 6 represented the days of Creation; 3 the Trinity; 7 the Creator, Holy Spirit, Grace of God; 12 the Apostles. Of special significance is the number 14. It represents the name Bach when the letters' numerical positions in the alphabet are added together (B flat-2, A-1, C-3, H(B natural-8), and its place in this Fugue is both intriguing and enlightening. The subject contains 14 notes. Not only does Bach choose a noble melodic motif to begin but also establishes his identity by the number of notes in the subject.

At the 14th bar a series of stretti begin that proceed to a magnificent stretto maestrale (bars 16–19) a rare form in which the subject is imitated in its entirety in all the voices. Additional power is given to this section by a 14th entry of the subject in the soprano (incomplete), which resounds with rich chords.

Within the theme are two prominent intervals of the fourth, an interval historically significant as a fundamental religious symbol. It is hardly surprising that Bach includes this as part of his identity. The combination of the rising scale and the leaping fourth is a striking characteristic in many of the C major melodies.

Now, amidst the strength and confidence displayed in the Fugue, in the bass at bar 16 appears a brief descending chromatic scale, a motif that always symbolizes sorrow and grief. It is placed strategically at the start of the stretto maestrale. It appears again in bar 24 in the soprano during the last subject entry. Being conscious of this motif in these passages increases the emotional impact. The coda is highlighted by a trumpet-like flourish (often found in the choruses in this key) that soars to the highest note in the composition, supported by an increase in voices. Glory and omnipotence.

Prelude, C Major, Book II

Using the signature rising scale over a resounding tonic octave in the bass, Bach leads us with stately grandeur into the second volume of the *WTC*. Instead of following the scale with intervals of the fourth, Bach now uses those of the sixth. Way back before Bach's time, the intervals of the third and sixth were not to be used in melodies. Influenced by the principles of acoustics of Pythagoras, which labeled them as "dissonances," they were considered "detested intervals." Bach made short shrift of that theory (though respectfully, no doubt) as we will see throughout the *WTC*. He invested the sixth with joy and often humor and gaiety. (See Fugue in E major, Book I.)

As a bud that unfolds to become a multipetaled flower, the opening solo bursts into bloom with four-part harmony where the broken chord, in an alternate note pattern with passing notes, is exploited to the fullest. The music develops complexity and abounds in skillfully crafted harmonic modulations, highlighted by chromaticism and in particular, by the inspired Neapolitan sixths at two climactic phrases (bars 11 and 26), both of which modulate to minor keys.

It is the turn that gives the unique character to this Prelude. It is the core of the melodic development. With two rhythmic patterns (♫♫♩ ♩ and ♫♫♫♫♫) it is the secret of the Prelude's charm and elegance.

The mordent also has a thematic role here. In the overall plan it not only adds its own radiance but will become the leading motif in the companion Fugue.

Then there are the descending chromatic passages. In the Book I Fugue in C major this symbol of grief and sorrow appears briefly in two places. Although unobtrusive, nevertheless its presence is felt. Indeed, Bach even includes it in this Prelude, giving the exact phrase to the tenor in bar 26. Prior to that, though, a much longer chromatic passage dominates the middle of the piece, intensified by elaborate harmonization. This motif within an otherwise expression of joy and affirmation has caused others to ponder its significance. One scholar has interpreted it as Bach being "pensive, inwardly musing, and occupied with the origin and end of humanity." Might it not also be that Bach is revealing a universal truth—in the cosmic scheme of things, joy and sorrow go hand in hand through life? The warp and weft of human experience.

With an increase of voices and a final, powerful, seven-note tonic chord, Bach concludes the Prelude with glowing confidence and strength.

Fugue, C Major, Book II

The descending chromatic scale has no place in this Fugue. It is jubilant from beginning to end.

The subject consists of 21 notes. Because the number 7 symbolizes the Holy Spirit for Bach, this then is three times holy, a musical translation of the letters S, D, G (Soli Deo Gloria), which he often put at the end of a major work.

The mordent, dancing with unbridled exuberance, appears more or less 43 times in 83 bars, depending on how many times you play it in the subject repetitions. Like the turn in the Prelude, this ornament is heard in two rhythmic patterns: ♫♩ and ♫♩..

With a leap of a sixth, a rhythmic joy motif (♫ ♫ ♩) and a succession of rapid notes (from which the countersubject is formed) this is surely a melody of rejoicing.

At bars 67–68 there is a drop of a major seventh in the bass at an inter-
rupted cadence. This is special. A singular example of the effect of this
melodic interval is found in the soprano aria *Mein gläubiges Herze* (My faithful heart, rejoice) from Cantata 68. In the final phrase she sings, "Dein Jesus
ist da" (Thy Jesus is here). By falling the seventh on the last two words her
joy is crowned with certitude. The melody also contains the rising fourth
and sixth and a mordent. There is a deep kinship between that aria and this
Fugue.

An increase of voices and wonderful chords herald the finale to Bach's
joyful Song of Praise.

2

C Minor

C minor is a strong key. Throughout the many compositions for which Bach chose this tonality, there is a feeling of composure and confidence. This is reflected particularly in several choral works where the theme of the text is patience in suffering, yet longing for release from life's troubles.

Bach left us a wealth of instrumental and choral music in this key, among which are: for keyboard, Invention no. 2, Sinfonia no. 2, Partita no. 2, French Suite no. 2, Toccata no. 3, a concerto for two harpsichords, an organ Prelude and Fugue (The Great), an organ Trio Sonata, and the monumental organ Passacalgia. For strings: a sonata for violin and clavier and a Suite for unaccompanied cello.

There are many great choral works, but I will single out three of the more familiar. In the solo Cantata 82, two of the three magnificent bass arias are in C minor—the first, *Ich habe genug* (I have enough) and the third *Ich freue mich auf meinen Tod* (I rejoice in my death). In each of the Passions Bach chose this key for only two of the numbers, each one a work of extraordinary power and beauty. In the *St. John Passion* they are the tenor aria *Erwäge* (Behold then), a testimony of triumph and grace through suffering, and the final chorus *Ruht wohl, ihr heiligen Gebeine* (Rest well, Beloved, sweetly sleeping). In the *St. Matthew Passion* they are also a tenor aria *Ich will bei meinem Jesu wachen* (I will watch by my Jesus), a testimony of steadfast devotion, and the final chorus *Wir setzen uns mit Tränen nieder* (We sit in tears of grief). That Bach would conclude both these Passions with choruses in C minor is of considerable spiritual significance.

Prelude, C Minor, Book I

This Prelude has all the improvisational character and style of a toccata. From the very first notes we know it is a dynamic and impressive piece. Bach has given tempo indications for the last three sections but not for the beginning. No doubt he assumed the player would be instinctively guided by the resonant texture of the music and perhaps the last Allegro means a return to the tempo of the first section. Among professional interpretations, there are as many different tempi as there are numbers between 66 and 116 on the metronome. One thing is certain—there must be a contrast between the first part and the Presto. And there are factors to take into consideration when choosing the most effective speed.

Bach did wonderful things with the broken chord, that important innovation in music that inspired creative ingenuity in a composer and displayed the skill of a performer. The first three Preludes in Book I are all based on this form. Here the basis is a broken chord incorporating a mordent in the pattern.

The driving power and the drama of the music lie in the harmonic progressions. This can be enriched on the piano by a slight emphasis on the first note of each group of 16ths in the treble, creating a melodic focal point, for as Spitta (*J. S. Bach*) pointed out, "The motive does not consist merely of a broken chord but has besides something of a melodic character." At strategic places one might choose to emphasize the bass notes for special melodic effect.

As the music unfolds Bach makes subtle changes in the motivic pattern. For 13 bars the first notes of the first and third groups is the highest and the first note of the second and fourth groups goes below the mordent. At bar 14 we see the first change. The "melodic" notes are all above the mordent.

That this change occurs at this particular point is not without special interest. We know that the number 14 represents Bach's name in numerical symbolism. In alphabetical placement B-2, A-1, C-3, H-8 = 14. It was a secret code in which Bach often identified himself in a piece—a kind of personal signature. There were several ways he did this, but three most commonly recognized are 14 notes in a theme, a particularly potent 14th entry of a fugal subject, or, as is the case here, something special happening in the 14th bar. From this moment until the Presto more rapid changes in the motif build the tension—bars 19–20 a reversal of "melodic" pattern in the soprano, bars 23–24 a return to the pattern of bar 14, all superbly calculated to heighten the effect of the arpeggiated approach to the Presto.

A slight ritard at the end of bar 27 allows a "change of gears" for the launch into the brilliant tour-de-force of the Presto. Now comes the real test of skill with difficult parallel motion, abrupt changes in pattern, and tearing speed. But what an impassioned and powerful climax!

The Adagio is and should sound improvisatory, free yet rhymically relative in note values—a spontaneous, reflective transition. Notice that Bach has written a mordent ornament in this passage, a final allusion to the basic motif of the Prelude.

The finale is grand and, with its deep resonant pedal-point, as imposing as the closing moments of one of the great organ works.

Fugue, C Minor, Book I

There is nothing ambiguous about the "affection," the emotional dimension, of this Fugue. The subject is a bold, confident statement and dominates the entire composition. The rhythmic pattern set forth in the first notes, ♫.♫♩, one of Bach's joy motifs, is a vital element, its spirit underscored by the fact it occurs 48 times within 31 bars.

The melody set to this rhythmic motif includes the mordent, which is the basis of the companion Prelude. Bach had a propensity to use certain melodic motifs repeatedly in pieces in C minor. The mordent is one of them. It is an important part of the themes of both the Prelude and Fugue in this key in Book II, and appears at the beginning of the second Invention and the last movement of the fourth harpsichord and violin sonata.

Perhaps the most revealing clue to its significance in terms of affect is found in choral works specifically written in this tonality. Two examples are particularly relevant in our search.

In the soprano and alto duet *Er kennt die rechten Freudenstunden* (He knows the right hours for joy) in Cantata 93, written in 1728—a time when Bach was often under considerable stress—the mordent occurs repeatedly in both the solo parts and the continuo. The theme of the text is patience in suffering, calm confidence, and steadfast faith.

In the magnificent soprano aria *Ich bitte dich, Herr Jesu Christ* (I ask Thee, Lord Jesus Christ) in Cantata 166, written in 1725, the mordent is the essential element both in the violin and viola part and in the continuo. The text theme is firm resolve to remain strong in confidence and faith.

Bach chose two countersubjects for this work, one a flowing descending scale and the other a melody of sedate steps. Both superbly counterbalance and enhance the angular subject melody. They also give Bach ample opportunity to display his expertise in double and triple counterpoint.

Notice the development in emotional dynamics through episodes three and four. The lovely undulating melody of the former begins benignly in E-flat major but moves through the darker color of F minor. This implication of increasing unease is realized in the latter. Bach builds considerable tension with deliberate dissonances of ninths and sevenths between the fourth note of the theme and the second note of the rising scale in bars 17 to 19. In addition, the bass line moves through ascending chromatic harmony—consistently symbolic in his music of intense inner conflict. He alluded to this conflict earlier in the piece in the ascending chromatic in the soprano in bars 5 and 6.

Now he must resolve this conflict. He does so by bringing the strong subject theme absolutely front and center right through the final section, the mordent motif making its most compelling statement in the climax in bars 25 and 26.

A final entry of the subject in the soprano, a resounding pedal-point octave in the bass, an increase of voices, and a resolute rhythm in the double alto voices in the final bar epitomizes the uncompromising character and inner strength of the great man himself.

Prelude, C Minor, Book II

There are many elements in this piece that relate directly to those in the same key in Book I. We immediately see that the mordent is once again the leading motif in the theme and a melodic focal point accompanies the motif as in the Prelude in the first book. The texture here is much lighter and has a beautiful lyrical quality. But Bach is still thinking of that first C minor Prelude. He has brought forward figurative passages directly from the Presto in the earlier work to bars 5, 6 and 7 in this piece, yet the character of the figures is subtly transformed by the different rhythmic and melodic context.

In the music of this Prelude there are intimations pointing to the deep emotional conflicts, which are expressed in the C minor choral works already listed. At bar 17 Bach has modulated to F minor, a key always associated with sorrow, and this is followed by two bars of descending chromatic harmony, also symbolic of pain and suffering. The tonality of F minor permeates through to bar 23. From here one senses inner strength returning and culminating in a powerful passage in the penultimate bar where two symbolic expressions of intense emotion occur—the ascending chromatic scale and the interval of the ninth. Both of these had an important place in the C minor Fugue in Book I. There, the ascending chromatic first appears early in the piece, then, combined with the ninths, in the highly charged middle section. Here too it is heard early in the piece at bar 4, and then is reserved for the climactic approach to the close, with the ascending chromatic in the bass and leaps of the ninth in the soprano resolving on a strong cadence with an increase of voices and a resolute (but purposely minor) final chord.

Fugue, C Minor, Book II

Bach concludes his *WTC* series of pieces in C minor with a reflective, serious Fugue, imbued with an aura of composed resignation, dignity and confidence. And, indeed, especially symbolic of Bach himself in his later years.

As would be expected, it has deep spiritual overtones. The subject consists of nine notes, which is a multiple of three, the symbolic number for the Trinity. C minor is, of course, the relative minor of the Trinity key E flat major and this relationship is underscored in the music. Within the melody is a prominant interval of the fourth—that fundamental religious symbol closely associated with the Trinity.

Also of special significance, Bach has included in the subject that cornerstone of the C minor pieces—the mordent, which then is formed twice in the answer. It is with this melodic motif that Bach has created a bond between all the pieces in C minor in the WTC.

We saw that he brought forward a melodic figure from the Prelude in the first book to the Prelude in the second book. Here he makes subtle allusions to the Fugue in the first book: In bar 3, the melody in the alto is reminiscent of the second countersubject in the earlier piece; in bar 4, the rhythmic figure of the soprano (♫ ♫ ♩) is like that of its subject; in the episode at bar 6 we hear the descending scale that formed its first countersubject.

There is no real countersubject in this Fugue. The emphasis is focused entirely on the subject, its depth of sentiment magnified by stretti, augmentation, and inversion.

An unusual feature of Bach's design is that this four-part Fugue is, for considerable length, in only three voices. Perhaps this is also a symbolic allusion to the Trinity. During this development of the Fugue all four voices are heard in various combinations, but until bar 19 they do not appear together. The theme is woven throughout this section with the touch of the master, its affect blending with flowing melodies, beautiful rhythmic patterns and harmonic and melodic sequences. Notice in particular the Neapolitan sixths in bar 11 (the G-flat in the modulation to F minor) and in bar 12 (the A-flat in the modulation to G minor).

In the C minor Prelude in Book I, I made reference to the number 14, which symbolically represents Bach's name, specifically in connection with the 14th bar. In this Fugue too, something special happens at bar 14—the subject appears in stretto with the theme in the first augmentation in the alto, which then is joined in the tenor with the theme in inversion. An important moment.

The awaited entry of all four voices is marked by an austere, imposing statement in the bass of the theme in augmentation. No other voices sing the theme during this climactic moment in the Fugue, but their melodies add immeasurably to the emotional intensity as the music approaches the final section.

The closing of the Fugue with its close stretti and organ-like cadenza is one of total affirmation, resonating with courage and certitude.

3

C-Sharp Major

The advent of mean-temperament tuning extended the range of tonality to include compositions in five, six, or seven sharps or flats. Also, unusual harmonic modulations within pieces in any key could be explored and, sometimes, daringly designed. These new keys inspired Bach to create for both volumes of the WTC works of extraordinary quality. They are all masterpieces.

All the pieces in C-sharp major contain material evincing a sense of joy, delight, and confidence. It is also clearly evident that they are a challenge to the player—brilliance, advanced technical skill, and dexterity have been imposed on a difficult key. To Bach, nothing was impossible. You just had to work diligently (his word). These four pieces are so wonderful; do take his advice. You will be amply rewarded.

Prelude, C-Sharp Major, Book I

The first three Preludes in Book I of the WTC exploit one of the important innovations in music—the broken chord. Indeed, the way the chords were broken became an art in itself. So many possibilities opened up for a composer, it proved fertile ground for the creative imagination, enriching both harmonic and technical effects. For the keyboard player it meant many new challenges in dexterity and skill. Bach, the master of this form, displays all of these things in this brilliant and dazzling Prelude.

The type of broken chord that Bach uses here was known at that time as *batteries*. This term is associated with the guitar, a striking of the strings rather than plucking them. What seems evident here is a Spanish influence, and in particular, the music of Scarlatti. It is certain that Bach was familiar with Scarlatti's sonatas and admired them. There was very little going on in the music world that Bach did not know about. Published music from France, Italy and Spain was brought to him by musician friends and connoisseurs. The Spanish spirit is most pronounced in the special *batteries* form beginning at bar 63 through to bar 96.

The spirited, dancing, pattern accompanying the batteries contains a special feature which is not to be missed. Highlighting the end of each eight-bar section is a leap down of an interval of the major seventh. It is an interval often associated in Bach's melodies with great joy. And we will see that he will give it prominence in the companion Fugue.

Whirlwind passages of 16th notes based on the turn build the excitement to fever pitch, flying out from the *batteries* like fireworks. That the motif of these melodies is the turn is significant, too, for it, along with the major seventh will go directly into the subject of the Fugue.

How else would Bach end such a jubilant piece but with a cadenza of arpeggios and climactic multivoiced solid chords!

Fugue, C-Sharp Major, Book I

You may have noticed that Bach did not write a fermata over the last chord of the Prelude. So, no lingering. Take a short breath on the rest and immediately (and bravely—seven sharps!) launch the Fugue on the upbeat.

Bouncing from the first note right into a whirling turn, skipping up to the E for the descending broken tonic chord that opened the Prelude and springing into leaps of intervals of the sixth, the whole subject establishes the exuberant gaiety which will pour forth from every bar of this Fugue.

Wherever we find several leaps of the sixth in Bach's music they invariably express humor and joy. They may also reflect Bach's expansion of keyboard technique by standardizing use of the thumb, which made large intervals easier to play.

The subject ends with that striking interval pointed out in the Prelude—the major seventh. An illuminating illustration of the character which Bach associated with this melodic idiom is found in the great soprano aria *Mein gläubiges Herze* (My faithful heart rejoice) in Cantata 68. The whole aria is an entreaty to rejoice and be merry. In the text the melody of her final words, "Dein Jesus ist da" (Thy Jesus is here) emphasizes her joy and certitude by a leap of a sixth and then a dramatic drop of the seventh.

It is this exact same melodic pattern that forms the end of this fugal theme and surely transmits the spirit of earthly happiness.

There are two countersubjects partnering this wonderful theme, both completely independent and unique. The first is a rollicking series of tumbling 16ths and the second a more sober and simple melody. The first is so like the whirling 16th melodies in the Prelude, infectious in their exuberance, and the second contrasting in its more restrained stepwise syncopated motion.

Humor, too, has its place in all this gaiety. Notice the dissonant ninth, sounding emphatically on a strong beat, between the theme and first countersubject in bar 4, and again on the third entry between bass and alto. It will appear often in the playful dialogue between the two themes. But not every time. After the third episode, in the alto entry at bar 19 that voice and the bass meet at bar 20 on a *major seventh*. Then, after the little fourth episode, at the soprano entry at bar 25, something very special occurs. Bach has written one of his rare dynamic indications—a P. Here the soprano and bass join at the third beat on an interval of a minor seventh (compound), but at bar 27 on the third beat, the tenor and soprano meet quietly and unobtrusively on an interval of a ninth. In keeping with the gentle mood, the passage cadences with the subject ending not with the drop of the major seventh, but rising a step up to the tonic note of C-sharp major.

Since leaps and jumps are such an important element in this Fugue, revel in those wild ones of a 12th in episode three (bars 16–18) and be thankful you don't have to sing them!

The episodes are filled with Bach's inimitable genius for creating with music the feeling of sheer and unbounded happiness. Broken triads in a rhythmic joy motif (♫ ♩/♫ ♪) leap-frog from one voice to another in episodes one, two, and six and virtually play tag with one another in episode five where part of the theme and *batteries* (drawn into the game from the Prelude) join in all the excitement.

Bach brings all this breathless merriment to a close with the last entry of the subject in the same voice at the same pitch as he began, includes the first countersubject but not the sedate second one, and weaves the last notes of the theme into the final jubilant multivoiced chords.

Prelude, C-Sharp Major, Book II

Bach originally wrote this Prelude in C major, but because he had begun the first book with a Prelude of similar character and mood, he simply transposed this one into C-sharp major. If anything, the music has been enhanced by the rarefied atmosphere of the ultimate tonality in the key system. I, for one, am eternally grateful he did not discard this Prelude. Is there anyone who has played it and not loved it from the first note nor been deeply affected by the harmonic beauty of the first section?

With its arpeggiated chords, embellished with passing notes, a hypnotically pulsating tenor line of melodic implications and tolling bass notes, the music epitomizes inner peace and contentment.

A small but significant detail that plays a subtle role in the overall effect is the constant syncopation of the top note of each broken chord. If we compare this to the C major Prelude in Book I, we see that there the highest note of the arpeggiated chord first sounds on the beat but then is echoed on the last 16th of the chord repetition. In this Prelude Bach uses only the syncopated form. A bell-like sound on this top note carries through the alto and tenor's melodic and rhythmic rocking figure. A rhythmic rocking figure is, mysteriously, a thread woven into all the other five- and six-sharp Preludes in Book II—B major, G-sharp minor, F-sharp major and D-sharp minor.

As though rousing from a blissful state of reverie in the first section (which is brought, significantly, to a cadence on the dominant key) the music suddenly bursts into a spontaneous and happy little waltz. Marked allegro by Bach, indicating a spirited rather than a very fast tempo, the fughetta is based entirely on one simple, jaunty melodic motif (and its inversion) and leaping dance steps.

It is unusual for Bach to combine two heterogeneous elements in a Prelude, but we can see his choice of moving to a dance form was truly inspired. The two distinct sections of the Prelude flow from one to the other in the most natural way from an emotional viewpoint. From sublime contentment to an irresistible urge to get up and dance. A beautiful musical expression of a moment of pure joy.

Fugue, C Sharp Major, Book II

What strikes us immediately is the seemingly common theme of the subject of this Fugue. But what is amazing is how genius develops a simple figure. We can compare this to a simple line drawn by an artist such as Paul Klee or Picasso that evolves into a brilliant, original design. Bach takes this broken chord through the gamut of contrapuntal possibilities—inversion, augmentation, diminution, and stretto. What is of the utmost importance, though, is the symbolic meaning of the motif and its affect. Widely separated intervals denote strength, confidence, and pride. As a natural progression from the contentment and joy expressed in the companion Prelude, the Fugue exhibits nothing less than a total sense of well-being. Inner strength is implicit not only in the spaced intervals of the chord but in the steps following, separated by a rest (♪ ♪ ♪ ♪ ♫♩). An example of this pattern and its meaning can be found in several Fugues in the collection, most notably the B-flat minor Fugue in Book II.

Bach used this form of the broken chord motif many times in both his instrumental and choral compositions. One of the truly momentous occasions is the chorus *Fecit potentiam* (He hath showed strength) in the *Magnificat*, the word *potentiam* gloriously highlighted by a spectacular trumpet part.

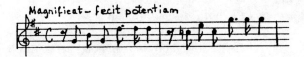

In the C-sharp major Fugue in Book I we noted a decisive element in its subject—the jubilant leaps. We now see that this element has become indigenous to the Fugues in this tonality, and Bach uses it here to make a continuous interpretation of joy.

Each voice is a marvel melodically and should be played often by itself. The alto, though, is a world unto itself, often unpredictable and daring. We felt the beauty of the syncopation in the companion Prelude. Syncopation abounds throughout this Fugue and is a major factor in the whole spirit of the piece but notice particularly three unique examples of it in the alto in bar 6, bars 12–13, and bars 22–23.

It is the alto, too, that is given the first of the two augmentations of the theme, ushering in the final section of the Fugue.

And what a culmination Bach has composed for the pieces in the ultimate tonality of the key system! Grand in every way with its increase of voices, quasi-cadenza flourishes, and stately, resounding, organ-like finale.

4

C-Sharp Minor

Apart from the Preludes and Fugues in C-sharp minor in the *WTC*, Bach confined his choice of this key to very few compositions. The Adagio in the violin and clavier sonata BWV 1016, the Siciliano in the clavier concerto BWV 1053, and the Adagio in the violin concerto BWV 1042 comprise the instrumental works. The bass aria (no. 2) in Cantata BWV 49, the soprano aria (no. 8) in Cantata BWV 210, and the tenor aria (no. 2) in Cantata BWV 8, are, to my knowledge, the sole instances in the choral works.

The predominant moods in these compositions can be described as introspective and contemplative, often suffused with intense longing and questioning. In whatever style Bach chose for each piece in this key, the emotional ambience is invariably expressed in music of deeply affecting beauty.

Prelude, C-Sharp Minor, Book I

Seldom has such depth of feeling and pathos been expressed more poetically in musical language than in this Prelude. Flowing melodic themes, richness of harmony, and exquisite transparent contrapuntal texture are combined to perfection.

The theme immediately evokes a pensive mood. Its crux is the leap up the octave through a rolled chord, a poignant cry subsiding stepwise in a gentle rhythm, then echoed in the tenor. Even more heartrending is the sequel, its higher pitch accentuated by a preparatory note rising a sixth. The tenor's reply to this sequel has a telling modification—a mournful rise of a minor seventh instead of an octave.

The sentiment implied in this theme can be discerned in two other pieces, where Bach used the same melodic figuration, and in keys which held for him related emotional associations—Invention no. 7 in the Passion key of E minor and Invention no. 9 in F minor.

These pieces reveal such a close relationship to the Prelude, I have wondered if Bach composed all three around the same time. Presumably the Prelude was the last—a consummate treatment of the thematic material which must have meant a great deal to him. While in the E minor Invention the theme is a key element in its beautiful melodic development, it is in the F minor Invention that we find the most direct affinity with the Prelude, where wide melodic leaps are crucial to the affect of both pieces. In the Prelude their effect, particularly that of the 9th, 10th and diminished 5th (or augmented 4th), is a wondrous combination of immediate and subliminal.

There is also one melodic figure of considerable significance that occurs in both pieces only once, and which Bach has specifically notated. This is the pair of slurred notes, the sigh motif, and a symbol of grief. Whereas in the Invention it appears early (bar 8), in the Prelude at bar 36 it is part of the emotionally charged diminished seventh harmonic progression leading to the final climax before the conclusion.

The spirit of the Prelude, though, emanates from the melodic motif that begins the theme. The beauty of this seemingly simple melody is continuously illuminated as the music flows through its harmonic and melodic journey. There is seldom a bar in which it does not appear in its original or slightly modified form.

The most daunting question one has to deal with in the Prelude is ornamentation. That it is a type of piece which traditionally called for embellishment is certain. In an earlier version Bach did not include ornaments. In a later version he added some, perhaps as a guide for his students. How much should be added extemporaneously? Landowska advocated liberal application, specifically those of French origin, saying that "without ornaments the piece is unintelligible" (*Landowska on Music*, pp. 183 and 390). Badura-Skoda, on the other hand, believes a much less embellished version "has a greater immediacy ... its noble arioso lines more moving..." (*Interpreting Bach at the Keyboard*, p. 486). Decisions on this important aspect of interpretation can only be reached through serious contemplation and perceptive awareness of the thoughts behind the creation of this exceptional Prelude.

I have been singling out important facets of this piece, but the greatness of a composition lies not in its details but in the realm to which they transport us through the genius of the composer.

Nowhere have I found the realm of this Prelude more movingly depicted than in the words of Cecil Gray, when he wrote,

> here we find ourselves in a world beyond joy or sorrow even.... At the very outset of the Prelude the recitative-like phrases, the solemnity of the melodic line are strongly reminiscent of the Passion Music of Bach ... Bach intoning a chant in which we catch an echo of the very incantation that

preceded Creation itself. It is a miraculous piece, of the utmost simplicity, so that any child could play it; at the same time there is in it a depth of meaning, a perfection of utterance, to which the greatest artist can hardly do justice (*The Forty-Eight Preludes and Fugues of Johann Sebastian Bach*).

Fugue, C-Sharp Minor, Book I

Bach now leads us from the Prelude to a Fugue of epic proportions. It is one of the longest, and the only one in the *WTC* in five voices with three subjects. The magnitude of the work cannot be grasped by its performance alone. It is the performer (as Bach intended in his title page) to whom it will be fully revealed through the intimacy of score and practical study, and awakened consciousness of the scope of the design, the prodigious contrapuntal mastery, and the power of the thematic and harmonic development.

The serious tone of the Fugue is established in the first subject. Bach actually already alluded to this theme in the opening of the Prelude—the tied C-sharp in the bass in bars 1–2 moving to B-sharp at bar 3, then the E in the soprano at the end of bar 3 and moving to D-sharp in bar 4. The tenor melody in the last bar also anticipates the Fugue's opening theme.

The figure of the subject forms a cross motif, which can be seen by drawing a line from the first note to the fourth and from the second to the third. It is a symbol of suffering and grief, underlined here by the interval of a diminished fourth in the melody. The most relevant and explicit case where Bach used this melodic figure in a choral work is the searing chorus *Lass ihn kreuzigen!* (Let him be crucified) in the *St. Matthew Passion*.

Adding a further dimension to the Fugue's theme, Bodky pointed out that "this subject contains a disguised allusion to the musical figuration B A C H" (*The Interpretation of Bach's Keyboard Works*). A symbolic inference of Bach's personal identification with this work.

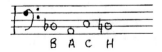

Bach's choice of voices for this Fugue is closely related to the theme, for the number 5 is also a symbol of the Crucifixion (the five wounds inflicted on Jesus), thus of suffering and pain.

Bach's plan that this be a triple Fugue adds considerably to the role symbolism plays in the scenario. The number 3 is the symbol for the Trinity, although its sacred attributes stem far back to ancient Greek philosophies. While being primarily represented by three subjects, Bach has woven this number into the whole fabric of his design.

The piece consists of three periods, the first to bar 35, the second to bar 73, and the third from there to the conclusion. In the exposition the subject first makes three entries, a short episode separating them from the fourth and fifth. This arrangement has further symbolic implications. The *fifth*, and highest voice, has been designated to enter in bar 14—the symbolic number for Bach's name. In many of the Preludes and Fugues we often find something significant occuring in the 14th bar. This is but one way Bach encoded his name numerically within a composition. A subject theme of 14 notes, or a particularly arresting 14th entry of a subject invariably indicates a personal association with the affect of the piece.

Returning to the number 3 in this first section, Bach has also represented it in multiple form, for there are nine entries of the subject. A further numerical multiple with related symbolic implications can be detected in the length of this section. Bach completed it at bar 35—a multiple of five and the definitive holy number, 7. But before reaching the 35th bar, he adds a 10th entry, in modified form, as part of a modulation which closes the section in E major. It is, of course, the relative major, but, being the sharpest and therefore the "highest" in common use, it was considered in the Baroque era as the "Key of Heaven." This symbolic attribute can be seen to have considerable bearing on the character of the second subject, which now makes its entrance.

The serenity and gentleness of this flowing melody, reminiscent in character of other melodies in Bach's work which have been identified as the "flight of angels," creates a sublime aura around the cross-motif theme. Again, number symbolism is present in the union of the two themes. They appear together three times before the third subject is introduced. Between the second and third, Bach interjects an episode at bar 41, the other number symbolic of his name (J S B A C H). It is marked as being the only time that the second subject appears in inversion. In addition, the length of this union of the first and second themes is 14 bars.

After the third statement of the first and second subjects together another episode, featuring the second melody, harmonically prepares the entrance of the third subject in the key of F-sharp minor. And a great entrance it is. The dynamic character of this third subject brings into the symbolic realm a spirit of exultation. When Bach used this melodic figure in his choral works, it was in the context of the triumph of happiness over sorrow. Two superb examples are the first chorus of Cantata BWV 21, *Ich hatte viel Bekümmernis in meinem Herze* (I had much worry in my heart), and the tenor and bass duet *Wie will ich mich freuen, wie will ich mich laben wenn alle vergängliche Trübsal vorbei!* (How I will rejoice, how I will be refreshed, when all passing afflictions are over!) in Cantata BWV 146.

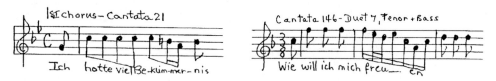

A very significant detail of this third subject is that it consists of seven notes. This most sacred of numbers was encoded in the first section, but now openly appears as the third in a trio of main symbolic numbers. We can be sure the particular moment this seven-note third theme enters is not coincidental. It is at bar 49, a multple of seven.

The next 24 bars celebrate the union of the three subjects. It is a passage marvelous in contrapuntal and harmonic beauty and a revelation of the perfection of Bach's thematic design.

The three symbolic numbers are again in evidence. The third entry of the three subjects has three distinctive elements. Bach has modulated to the Trinity key of A major. Accordingly, the first subject appears in a tonally modified form. It is with this special form, and in this special key, that stretto makes its first appearance in the music.

As in the first section of the Fugue, Bach separates these three entries of the first subject (in effect, a third and fourth entry) from its next entry by two bars.

During these two bars a small part of the second subject is heard in stretto. The fifth entry of all three subjects is marked by a return to C-sharp minor. Bach adds a sixth entry only for the second and third subjects. This is followed by an entry of the third subject alone, its seventh, and its turn to appear in stretto.

Notice particularly the approach to the cadence of this passage. In the opening of the Prelude we saw an allusion to the first theme of the Fugue. Now Bach makes an allusion to the Prelude in the tenor melody in bar 71, made all the more poignant by the harmonically chromatic descending accompaniment. Thus Bach indicates an emotional thread uniting the two pieces. Along with this, there is, in the notes A-sharp A-natural/B-sharp B-natural in bars 70–71 an allusion to his name.

Although in three periods, the Fugue is clearly subdivided in five sections. The third period now begins with a resounding declamation. In the next 21 bars, the fourth section, the three themes reach the zenith of their journey together. The approach to the culminating point is particularly beautiful with modulations through A major to F-sharp minor with the third subject in stretto and, at bar 89, the tenor once again singing the melodic motif of the Prelude. Above it the first subject begins the return to the tonic key. The section ends with the third subject ringing out at its highest pitch, while the second subject (the "angelic" presence) completes its role in the affect of the Fugue, exiting to leave the fifth and final section to the cross motif and the exultant spirit of the third subject.

Bach begins this magnificent finale with stretto in both themes, a device that sets the stage for the coalescence of their dynamic symbolic relationship, and culmination in the ultimate climax and triumphant conclusion. A climax and conclusion so reminiscent, in rhythm, tonal texture and harmonic power, of the great B-flat minor Prelude in Book I.

As a final tribute to this great Fugue, no words can surpass those of Spitta when he wrote, "It is one of the grandest creations in the whole realm of clavier music ... a composition of such vast breadth and sublimity, of such stupendous—almost overwhelming—harmonic power that Bach himself has created but few to equal it" (*J. S. Bach*).

Prelude, C-Sharp Minor, Book II

This Prelude is, in effect, an extended aria of poignant melodic beauty illuminated by exquisite contrapuntal treatment. Like the Prelude in this key in the first book, this too is in a style in which ornamentation plays a major role. Whereas in the earlier piece Bach left a great deal to the player's discretion, in this piece he has clearly indicated his intentions. One ornament that causes some uncertainty is the appoggiatura. When should it be long or short? Bodky suggested a general approach—"all before ♩. and ♩ need a length of ♪, before ♪. use ♪ " (*Interpretation of Bach's Keyboard Works*). In most cases this seems the most natural choice in the context of the melody. Another is the old polemic—should the trill begin on the note or the one above it? Research and study provide guidelines to this complex area of Baroque style, but the ultimate goal is to adorn the melodies skillfully and with the utmost musicality to enhance the beauty of the music.

The melodic figure that begins the aria conveys the essence of the mood which will pervade the whole development, harmonically and melodically. It rises through the spiritual symbol of a fourth to the minor sixth then falls to the fifth—an intervalic progression historically associated with sorrow. We find in two of the arias in this key, Bach used this figure, or one closely allied with it, in relevant, and revealing, contexts. One is the moving bass aria *Ich geh' und suche mit Verlangen* (I go and seek with longing) in Cantata BWV 49—Jesus in search of the soul. The other, equally affecting, is the tenor aria *Was willst du dich, mein Geist, entsetzen* (Why wilt thou be afraid, my soul) in Cantata BWV 8—an exhortation not to fear death.

Two further compositions, this time for clavier, show an adaptation of the figure in other tonalities where Bach signifies his intended affect through the intrinsic implications of this motif as an opening statement. One is the Prelude in E-flat minor in Book I and the other the Sinfonia no. 5 in E-flat major, where the entry of the motif, as in this Prelude, is prepared by a rising four-note form chord.

The rising broken chord is also an important motif that has actually evolved from the rolled form in the Prelude in Book I. It is heard five times in the bass at decisive cadences. This number, a symbol of sorrow and grief, was prominently represented in the Fugue in this key in Book I. Of related significance, the *St. Matthew Passion* begins with this melodic figure.

Its first appearance in the soprano (bar 27) marks a very special moment in the Prelude. The music has modulated to E major, the "key of heaven," and the broken chord prepares the entry of the third melodic motif. This motif with its repeated notes is a vestige of the third subject of the Fugue in Book I, now transformed from one of aggressive character to one with lilting charm. It is also of special interest that the first six notes of this melody are identical to those that begin the Prelude in E major in Book I— a piece of infinite charm and beauty.

Returning to number symbolism for a moment, we mentioned in the Fugue in Book I how Bach often encoded his name through the number 14 as a kind of personal identification with the music. Here, as in the Fugue, it is at the 14th bar where something noteworthy occurs. A resonant extended trill passage in the bass appears for the first time. Although trills occur during the course of the music, this particular extended form appears only three times, a symbolic number with spiritual associations also prominent in the Fugue. Significantly, the third instance has been reserved for the beautiful cadential approach to the conclusion of the piece. This number also appears in the beautiful modulation to F-sharp minor, a key associated with suffering. This occurs at bar 33, and it is here that the alto begins the third statement of the first theme, and the second section of the Prelude begins.

With lyrical tenderness the F-sharp minor passage leads the music back to the tonic key and to the fourth and last entry of the first theme. An ensuing series of descending chromatic steps in the soprano extend the affect of this theme. At its lowest point, the third theme rises in a surge of emotional intensity augmented by reiteration in the alto and bass. Reverberations of this climactic supplication filter down to the coda. With a stabilizing rising fourth in the bass, echoed in the soprano, the final moment of this beautiful elegy moves through the gentlest of climaxes to a meditative minor cadence where the last notes in the soprano presage the opening of its companion Fugue.

Fugue, C-Sharp Minor, Book II

A restless, turbulent Fugue. Although in the form of a gigue, three factors govern the affect of the piece: the time signature—triplets in 16ths played more lightly than those in 8ths and flowing without accents; the descending chromaticism—symbolically associated with sorrow or distress; and complex harmony—the heart and soul of the music.

Though seeming incompatible as a companion to the Prelude, it is inconceivable that Bach would complete his set in this key with a Fugue which has no relationship with the other pieces or has not evolved in spirit from them. In fact, he has incorporated elements from the two Preludes into this Fugue, which establish an intentional link.

Another factor to consider in forming a perception of the character of this piece is Bach's use of triplet 16ths in combination with descending chromaticism in the Fugue in D minor in Book II. The dramatic, serious tone of that music is not without parallel here. The critical difference in this Fugue is that the descending chromaticism is a distinct entity, forming part of a second subject.

Whatever intimation of inner peace and comfort arrived at by the end of the Prelude is swept away by the surging restlessness of the first subject of this double Fugue. This change is made more evident by the answer entering before the first statement is finished, and continued during the course of the music. It is as though the questions and seeking to understand the nature of suffering and sorrow posed in the other pieces continue to torment. The character of the thematic material, complexity of the counterpoint, incessant harmonic modulations (in one episode alone Bach sweeps through eight keys), and specific figurative language, all combine to create an extraordinary, vivid depiction of inner turmoil.

A key element of the language is angular leaps, one of the features of both Preludes, and used here in abundance, often with piercing effect. We hear the first right at the beginning in the drop of the major seventh from the leading note in the bass during the answer. Especially vital is the leap up a minor seventh in the soprano for the entrance of the second subject at bar 35. The all-imporant moment of the union of the two subjects at bar 48 is prepared in an intense passage during which the soprano makes many leaps of which the rising major seventh and the climactic octave just prior to the double entry demand special emphasis.

Focusing now on the specific moment Bach brings the two subjects together, we find a symbolic link to the Fugue in Book I and the companion Prelude to this Fugue. It is the secret intimation of the composer's personal identification with the affect of the music through the number 14, detected in both those pieces. Bach has designed the exposition of the second subject (beginning at bar 35) and the building of emotional intensity through the ensuing episode to encompass 13 bars. At the 14th bar the two subjects enter together. Adding to the symbolic significance of this pivotal event, he has modulated to the 14th key of the tonal system, F-sharp minor.

The dynamic interaction of the characters of the two subjects is the force that propels the final section of the Fugue to an impassioned, exclamatory ending. When Bach designed this final section, he was thinking of it not only as the climactic conclusion of this Fugue but of all the pieces in the group. This intimation is revealed by the inclusion of melodic figures from both Preludes. The first, although a figure already heard in earlier episodes in bars 59–60 is, in form, closely related to bars 5–7 in the Prelude in Book I.

The second, from both the first and the companion Prelude, is the rising broken chord in bar 65, which prepares the penultimate entry of the second subject.

In the concluding six bars the two subjects join in an uncompromising last statement, but it is the descending chromatic theme which, in pitch and number of entries, dominates the tone of this statement. Two accented drops of a diminished seventh in the bass following the last chromatic melody sustain the tension and underline the significance of an abrupt cadence to this powerful Fugue.

5

D Major

When Bach chose the key of D major, his focus was invariably on the spirit of gladness and its manifold expressions in life. It ranges from exaltation to triumphant and celebratory rejoicing to a serene sense of inner well-being and regal dignity. Often there is great wit and humor. There are no tears—unless they are tears of joy. Whether he is communicating privately, as in the *WTC*, or through his public works, the essence is the same.

What wonderful D major instrumental compositions he gave us: Invention no. 3, Sinfonia no. 3, a clavier concerto, the fourth of the *Twelve Little Preludes*, the fourth of the *Six Little Preludes*, Partita no. 4, a clavier toccata, an unaccompanied cello suite, an organ Prelude and Fugue, Brandenburg Concerto no. 5, and Orchestral Suites nos. 3 and 4.

Many of his most glorious works are choruses and arias in this key, among which the following are unsurpassed in beauty, grandeur and emotional impact: the opening choruses of Cantata 148 *Bringet dem Herrn Ehre seines Namens* (Bring to the Lord the honour of His name), Cantata 149 *Man singet mit Freuden vom Sieg* (One sings with the joy of victory), Cantata 80 *Ein feste Burg ist unser Gott* (A mighty fortress is our God), Cantata 215 *Preise dein Glücke, gesegnetes Sachsen* (Praise your good luck, blessed Saxony), the soprano aria *Et Exsultavit* in the *Magnificat*, and the great choruses in the *B minor Mass*—*Osanna, Gloria in excelsis, Cum Sancto Spiritu, Et resurrexit* and the monumental *Sanctus*. On the lighter side, D major finds its niche in marvelous arias in the comic *Peasant and Coffee Cantatas*.

Prelude, D Major, Book I

This much-loved Prelude, like the first three in the volume, displays Bach's skillful and imaginative treatment of the broken chord—this time ornamented with passing notes. It originally appeared in the Clavierbüchlein for Friedemann and expanded to create a virtuosic ending. It has all the improvisational character and brilliance of a little toccata.

The music dances like sunbeams on rippling water and sparkles with wit. Full of energy and joie de vivre, the left hand leaps and bounces, propelling the right-hand figurative melody into a flurry of twists and turns. A great deal of the humor comes from the dissonant harmony. I call it "teasing" dissonance—always begging for resolution. Look for lots of accented seconds between the hands. The modulations are as fleeting and ephemeral as the flight path of a butterfly, landing on a key for only a few seconds.

Excitement begins to build at bar 25, gaining momentum as the bouncing bass, over an added dominant pedal-point, rushes headlong in melodic duet with the soprano. All these wild antics are reined in by the sudden syncopation in bar 32, and all comes to a halt on a dramatic arpeggiated diminished chord. With a grand improvisational flourish of scales and arpeggios, Bach closes the piece—and, I think, breaks into laughter. The trick is to play this challenging little Prelude in the same spirit and laugh with him at the end.

Fugue, D Major, Book I

When we consider the affection of each of these D major pieces, it is not difficult to discern a relationship as the music evolves from the Prelude to its companion Fugue. The Prelude has all the excited anticipation of a forthcoming special event. The regal tone of the Fugue, complete with heralding trumpets, suggests that this is indeed a momentous occasion—perhaps a visit of a royal personage or a ceremony honoring civic dignitaries. A cause for celebration and rejoicing.

It is clear the Fugue is in the style of a French overture. In fact, the rhythm of the subject is almost identical to the opening of the fourth Partita, which Bach titled "Ouverture." And, as such, it fits perfectly the context of the imagined scenario.

The subject makes a grand entrance, imperial in every way. Its character and dynamics have always brought to my mind a spectacular entrance I once saw the great Russian ballerina Maya Plisetskaya make, bursting from the stage wings, flying through the air in breathtaking defiance of gravity. Her preparation for this leap must have been similar to the thrust of energy that propels the opening melody of the subject up to the dotted rhythm section.

This opening melody of the theme is a paramount motif throughout the piece, not only appearing in 11 subject entries but in the episodes as well—in all, a total of 34 times in 27 bars! And doubled the last three times—reminiscent of the whirlwind duet near the end of the Prelude. It is a melody of considerable significance for we find that Bach later used it in varying forms in choral works, always in association with happiness and gratitude. In Cantata 36 (1731) *Schwingt freudig euch empor* (Raise yourselves up joyfully), it forms the glorious opening of the first chorus.

Also from 1731, in Cantata 29 *Wir danken dir Gott* (We thank Thee, God), Bach presents this melody in the first chorus. This latter form of the theme, and indeed the whole chorus, must have held a special place in Bach's heart, for he transferred it to two great choruses in the *B minor Mass*—the *Gratias agimas* (We give thanks to Thee) and *Dona nobis pacem* (Grant us peace).

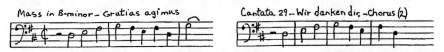

There is another element in this theme that is important. The transition from the opening melody to the dotted rhythm melody is always a leap of a sixth, an interval Bach used often, and in particular, several times in a piece when he wanted to express joy.

Although there is no regular countersubject in the Fugue, Bach introduces in the codetta between the second and third entries of the subject, a motif of equal prominence. Since it appears 19 times in the episodes, he has obviously assigned it an important role. It is an elegant little melody, always combined with the trumpet-like figure, lending much pomp and stateliness to the ceremonial pageantry.

A notable feature that distinguishes the unconventionality of this Fugue is the placement of the last statement of the subject. It comes well before the end and not even in the tonic but in the rather solemn key of E minor. Bach devotes the whole final section to glorifying the opening melodic motif, its symbolic connotation fervently affirmed in the closing bars.

Prelude, D Major, Book II

If the D major Fugue in the first book announces the impending arrival of the royal entourage or civic dignitaries, this Prelude celebrates the ceremonial event itself with triumphant and joyful music.

The rising D major chord proclaims the call to rejoice. Bach used this figuration definitively in the brilliant first chorus of Cantata 120 *Gott, man lobet dich in der Stille zu Zion* (God, one praises Thee in the stillness of Zion), which he wrote for the centenary celebration of the Augsberg Confession June 26, 1730. With the words *Jauchzet, ihr erfreuten Stimmen* (Rejoice, you joyful voices) the music urges the crowds of people to express their happiness in song. Interestingly, Bach later repeated this as the Ratswahl cantata on the election of civic dignitaries.

Even later he returned to this theme and adapted it for the *Et expecto resurrectionem* in the *B minor Mass*.

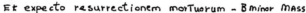
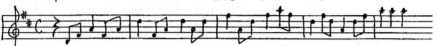

Is there not this same jubilant feeling captured in the opening bars of the third harpsichord concerto?

Mozart, too, evokes elation and joy by beginning his D major Sonata K576 with the rising tonic chord.

Trumpets and drums (outstanding in the chorus mentioned above) are all part of the scenario here just as they were in the Fugue in Book I, with the ♪.♫ figure the symbolic link between the two pieces. This figure forms an important melodic motif, which is first heard in bar 5, and appears strategically throughout the piece. It is the drop of the octave, which may be symbolically meaningful. It has been established as a Sanctus symbol (from the *B minor Mass*). Indeed, Bodky described this Prelude as a "majestic instrumental Sanctus," and ascribed the words "Praise the Lord" to the rhythmic/melodic figure in which the octave appears in the bass. On the other hand it does have a drum-like character. Certainly, Bach intended it to be an imposing and resounding motif.

A most unusual feature in this work is, of course, Bach's decision to write two time signatures. It is an ingenious solution (practical, too, when you think about it), when the music is dominated by both triple and duple rhythm. It allows both independence of the rhythms and syncronized combination as well. And a moment of polyrhythm at the beginning of the second section. Notice that Bach never writes a ♩., the pulse beat is ruled by the 𝄵 time signature.

There has always been (and probably always will be) a debate about whether the 16th note in the rhythm ♩.♪ should be played after the third note of a triplet when they occur together. In most cases it is played as C. P. E. Bach instructed in one of his essays—the dotted note is assimilated with the triplet. But Quantz maintained the short note should be played after it. Otherwise "the expression would be lame and insipid, rather than brilliant and majestic" (Quantz, *On Playing the Flute*, p. 68). These last words describe the character of this Prelude, and some interpreters have followed Quantz's advice judiciously with very convincing and effective results. It is certainly worth thinking about.

The recapitulation in this early sonata-form Prelude brings the glorious celebration to a fitting close, the jubilant spirit heightened with brilliant imitation passages. Six times the resounding falling octave rings out—the last time in regal emphasis in the final cadence.

Fugue, D Major, Book II

Bach concludes the set in D major with music that contrasts the celebratory and triumphant mood of the previous pieces with that of a more serene character. The Fugue, vocal in style, conveys a feeling of confidence and contentment with blessings bestowed on all those gathered for the special occasion.

The subject consists of nine notes, a multiple of the number three, an important symbol in Bach's music representing the Trinity. The rhythm of the subject (𝅘𝅥𝅮♩♩♩ ♩♩♩♩♩♩) also has special connotations. Bach used it in many cantatas and chorales in several variants to express feelings of happiness, in particular those associated with the promise of blessings bestowed on the faithful. One example is the accompaniment to the tenor aria *Sei getreu ... nach dem Regen blüht der Segen* (Be faithful ... after the rain blooms the blessing) in Cantata 12.

Cantata 12 – Bass aria – Sei getreu

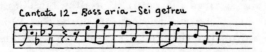

Adding further to the uplifting tone of the subject, the second motif contains the melodic rising interval of the fourth—a fundamental religious symbol closely associated with the Trinity. (Note the prominence of this interval in the Prelude in Book I in the Trinity key of E-flat major.) This motif forms the very heart of the music. Not only does it appear in 23 entries of the subject, Bach also made it the countersubject. It occurs over 80 times in the piece.

This magnificent work is a quintessential stretto fugue. It is a marvel of workmanship. Even for Bach, whose powers of concentration must have been prodigious, solving the contrapuntal problems would undoubtedly have demanded intense effort. Not the least would be avoiding monotony when the emphasis is on the device of repetition. Yet Bach's aim was always higher than technical mastery. At the forefront was the "affection." Everything—structure, rhythm, harmony and melodic motifs—was directed toward the expression of this emotional dimension. Repetition and stretto of the theme are the principal vehicles, but notice the insertion of rhythmic joy motifs (♫♩♩), especially the double one at the exquisite modulation to F-sharp minor, and the powerful descending scale at the climax in episode four.

Now comes the full emotional impact of the piece. In a glorious finale enriched with chromatic harmony and a grand stretto maestrale, that rare form of stretto where all the voices state the theme in succession (here at the smallest possible interval), Bach closes with 10 statements of the rising fourth motif crowned in the final bar with the tenor singing it with a rising fifth and a resolute low D in the bass. All inimitably designed to impart confidence and assurance.

6

D Minor

46

Bach wrote prolifically in the key of D minor, and a number of these works are designed to create considerable emotional impact. Several are bravura pieces demanding expert technical skill and command of the instrument. The mood is often dark, depicting anger, aggression (sometimes threatening), inner turmoil or brooding melancholy. Beethoven and Mozart interpreted this key with similarly characteristic music. Whatever the venue, Bach's world in D minor is always dramatic.

Some of the most notable of Bach's works in this key are, for keyboard: the Chromatic Fantasy and Fugue; the sixth English Suite; the first French Suite; the second Toccata; a harpsichord concerto; a concerto for three harpsichords; two organ Toccatas and Fugues—the "Dorian" and the universally famous BWV 565; for strings: a Suite for solo cello; a Partita for solo violin with its monumental Chaconne; a concerto for two violins, and in a class by itself, his crowning work, the *Art of the Fugue*.

Among the choral works are two angry, threatening choruses in the *St. John Passion*—no. 23 *Wäre dieser nicht ein Übeltäter* (If this man were not a malefactor) and no. 29 *Nicht diesen, diesen nicht* (Not this man, no, not him) and a plaintive alto aria *Von den Stricken meiner Sünden* (From the tangle of my transgressions). In the *St. Matthew Passion* we find the mocking, threatening chorus *Gegrüsset seist du, Judenkönig!* (Hail, King of the Jews!) and the heavily burdened bass aria *Komm süsses Kreuz* (Come sweet Cross). In Cantata 90 Bach surely meant to fill the congregation with fear and trembling with the D minor tenor aria *Es reifet euch ein schrecklich Ende* (There ripens for you a dreadful end) referring to the day of judgment.

The WTC Preludes and Fugues in this key are much more benign than these choral examples, but each has its own distinctive atmosphere of drama.

Prelude, D Minor, Book I

This Prelude originally appeared in a shorter form in the *Notebook for Friedemann*, compiled in 1720. Bach added the section from bars 15–26 thus advancing the technical level and expanding the emotional dimension for inclusion in the WTC.

Bach's design for the Prelude is another example of his ingenious treatment of the broken chord, which was such an important innovation in the development of keyboard writing, and which forms the basis of the first three Preludes in Book I of the WTC.

A somber, agitated mood is immediately established by the drum-like repeated notes in the bass. This is a device which Bach used to begin both the *St. Matthew* and the *St. John Passions* and which he used at the start of the alto aria *Von den Stricken meiner Sünden*, mentioned in the introduction to this key. The implication of the motif is clear in the contexts of these works and can be interpreted comparably in the opening of this Prelude.

That the piece is composed almost entirely of broken triads compels us to look closely at how Bach has done this in such a way that the emotional and dramatic impact is created and sustained. One of the factors is, of course, the driving force of the relentless triplet rhythm. Then there is the tremendous energy of the bass part—do not overlook the possibilities for dynamic phrasing and tonal emphasis in this part. Glenn Gould, in particular, creates very exciting effects in his interpretation. Another is the flow of the harmonic progressions, rapidly moving through minor, major, augmented and diminished chords. Indeed, right at the beginning, in a great undulating surge, the music wells up to the highest climactic note of the piece—the high C in bar 4—then subsides to the cadence at F major. From then on the tension seethes like great tidal waves in the midst of a storm.

A more subtle technique is involved in the arrangements of the broken chord so that "melodic interest" is woven into the patterns. Equally fascinating is the fact that these "melodies" are rhythmically varied so that they are formed on the third notes of a series of triplets, or on the second notes, creating an unsettling syncopated effect. At other moments the "melody" is on the first notes of the triplet. In bars 10, 11 and 12, at the start of the third section, all three of these variants occur.

In the midst of the broken chords, Bach has specifically inserted decisive elements to heighten the effect—the plunging four-note-form-chord in bar 13 and hurtling descending scales in bars 18 and 19. In bar 23 he reinforces his approach to the ending with the striking of two solid intervals of the sixth, rising in pitch to the climax. The descending chromatic scale is always associated with distress, grief, or pain. But a series of nine diminished chords descending chromatically, very daring at that time, is certainly a powerful depiction of turmoil. Yet what could be a stronger symbol of inner strength than the commanding, positive, cadence to this restless Prelude?

Fugue, D Minor, Book I

Landowska describes this Fugue as "sombre and authoritarian" (*Landowska on Music*, p. 184). Spitta thought it "bitter and capricious, as the composer's humour could be at times" (*J.S. Bach*). The common element expressed in both these opinions is the presence of a dark shadow hovering in the background.

The subject does give an impression of an aggressive or threatening mood. The slur, the stroke note, and the trill are all authentic instructions by Bach himself. The stroke sign, in his time, indicated a sharp marcato sound detached from both the note before and after, and, in this case, accentuated by the leap of the sixth, demands a forceful attack on the trilled note.

The Fugue in E minor Book II, a key (in Bach's works) related to D minor in many aspects, has a subject akin in mood and temperament to that of this Fugue. It, too, has a similar motif in 16th notes leading to aggressive stroke notes. An example of language patterns used with particular purpose.

After establishing the aggressive character right at the beginning, Bach goes on to reinforce this continually with many unusual and daring progressions, such as those in bars 16, 17 and 18. Harmonic clashes abound throughout the piece. The triple semi-tonal clash of G, G-sharp, and A in bar 18 is stunning—unprecedented in that period and, indeed, looking far into the future.

Throughout the D minor tonality there are many thematic idioms running like a thread through the various compositions. A scale rising from the tonic, which begins this fugal subject, was also chosen by Bach to begin Invention 4, the D minor harpsichord concerto, and the Presto of the D minor Toccata. Strong and imperious in all four instances.

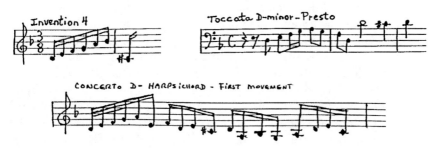

Within the little melody of 16th notes in the subject of this Fugue is a motif that Bach used in the theme of the D minor Sinfonia. A motif central to both pieces yet distinctive in character and musical affect.

The countersubject also has an imposing character, with its abrupt leap of the sixth and, especially, in the melodic motif with the repeated note. The conjunction of the repeated-note motif with the stroke note and trilled note of the subject in the exposition is certainly an unambiguous, forceful statement. Bach goes even further with a fourth entry of the subject, increasing the dynamic effect with double sixths on the stroke note and trill above the strong motif and repeating this twice in sequence. We heard the emphatic solid sixths at the end of the Prelude. They surely foretold the importance of this interval for the emotional intensity Bach wanted maintained through the companion Fugue.

Decisive as the subject is for the interpretation of this piece, we should not underestimate the significance of the repeated-note motif. The fact that Bach created a similar melody for one of the main themes of Contrapunctus 8 in *The Art of the Fugue* is very revealing, even more so when we see that the pattern appears again as the second countertheme of Contrapunctus 11—this time with BACH incorporated in the theme.

Bach's masterful contrapuntal skill is brilliantly displayed throughout the Fugue—the intricate weaving of all the motivic material between the voices, the powerful harmonic structure and, particularly, the stretti of the subject, the subject and its inversion, and the inversion. The appearance of the double thirds in the approach to the climax, as well as his adamant reiteration of the first motif of both the subject and its inversion, is of major importance in realizing the intense emotional experience Bach intended from the beginning. The penultimate bar with both the subject and inversion motif in contrary motion double thirds confirms the character of the piece. This is Bach, who, we know, was often combatant, strong-willed, a fighter against injustice, speaking clearly.

Prelude, D Minor, Book II

This is a dynamic Prelude, virtuosic and highly dramatic, seething with tremendous energy. It is galvanized into motion with a descending tonic scale, made all the more powerful by the descending octave in the bass— the Sanctus symbol, its meaning established in the Sanctus of the *B minor Mass*. (For more detailed discussion of this symbol, see Prelude in A-flat major, Book II.)

There are other pieces in D minor that open with the descending tonic scale, a decisively chosen motif, consistently indicative of the dramatic character of the music which will unfold. Two in particular are the third movement of the D minor harpsichord Concerto and the D minor organ Toccata BWV 565. Bach also expressly included this motif in *The Art of the Fugue*, where he incorporated it in a theme that combines with the principal theme in Contrapunctus 9.

I have twice mentioned the D minor harpsichord Concerto, relating it to the rising scale motif in the D minor Fugue in Book I and the descending scale in this Prelude, but there is further affinity with that Concerto. There are the *batteries* in bars 18 to 25 and in the final section of the

Prelude, and from bar 64 through to bar 81 in the first movement of the
Concerto and from bar 86 through to 99 in the third movement.

The sonority of the interlocked cross-voicing between the hands is
deeply affecting in both compositions. Then there is the rhythmic pattern
♫♫♫, a vital element throughout the first movement of the Concerto and
a catalytic interpolation in the first set of *batteries* in the Prelude.

Everything in this piece points to a raging internal storm of emotions.
Listen to the wild leaps in the chromatic harmony of bar 37 and the almost
frightening rising chromaticism in the scale in bar 40. This latter passage
always seemed to me a crucial moment in the piece, and in searching through
Bach's choral works, I found that he did indeed use the rising chromatic scale
to create intensely emotional scenarios. One such instance is in Recitative no.
73 in the *St. Matthew Passion*, where the Evangelist describes the cataclysmic
events following the Crucifixion. The opening of the graves and the rising of
the saints is pictorially depicted by a turbulent ascending chromatic bass line.

From this apex of the "storm" it is as though its fury gradually plays itself out and in the final bars, not unlike Beethoven's storm in the Pastoral Symphony, we hear the thunder rumbling in the distance.

This is a powerful Prelude demanding emotional intensity and technical expertise for its realization.

Fugue, D Minor, Book II

It is intriguing that the melody of the first half of the subject of this Fugue is intimately related to the theme of the D minor Fugue in Book I. Not only do both themes begin with the same four notes of the rising scale, but most of the theme of the Book I Fugue is woven into this melody.

Another interesting observation is that the subject of the Fugue in the first book consists of 12 notes and appears 12 times, and that this subject in the second book consists of 24 notes (a multiple of 12). It is also significant that the main theme of *Art of the Fugue* is a melody of 12 notes. The number 12 symbolically represented in Bach's works the church or the Apostles, and, by inference, personal faith. It has been identified in many of his compositions.

Other symbolic numbers are included in this Fugue. The rising interval of the fourth, a fundamental religious symbol, is conspicuous in the theme. The subject appears as real entries seven times—seven being, from ancient times, a "holy" number. Considering the character of the D minor pieces in the *WTC*, it is worth contemplating the meaning of these symbolic numbers and probing their role in them.

From the subliminal agitation of the final bars of the Prelude, the Fugue erupts with an intense upward surge of triplets, climaxing with a leap of a fourth then falling chromatically back to the tonic. This descending chromatic scale, historically associated with pain and grief, will be the dominant motif in the Fugue.

The emotional turmoil felt so strongly in the Prelude has not really disappeared in this companion Fugue, but has penetrated to a deeper level, a more private struggle evolving perhaps into a supplication for strength and compassion in the midst of anguish and distress.

There is inherent opposition and conflict between the triplet 16ths and those of the same value in groups of two. Bach does not directly pit these two rhythms against each other anywhere in the piece except in one instance—the cadence that closes the exposition, creating overt tension with the syncopation and polyrhythm.

This rhythmic configuration of triplets and duplets is another of the D minor *WTC* themes which Bach included in the *Art of the Fugue*—as the theme of Contrapunctus 13.

The descending chromatic motif never appears with the triplets either. Its poignancy is revealed and emphasized by being accompanied by the beautiful flowing duplet 16ths of the countersubject in the exposition. In a particularly moving passage during the fifth entry, the alto joins the soprano with its own descending chromatic melody rhythmically designed in a series of sigh motifs, which continue to sink to lower depths while the soprano suddenly leaps an octave, accentuating the anguish through a piercing reiteration of the chromatic motif.

The number 14 is also an important symbol. It represents the numerical value of the letters of Bach's name and is a kind of personal signature or identification. It appears in various guises and invariably at strategically important moments in his compositions. In this piece, it is at the 14th bar that he begins a magnificent stretto in which the chromatic motif of the subject in the soprano is greatly extended, and the alto, in its extension, again forms a series of sigh motifs beneath it. This leads to the dramatic entry of the inversion of the subject, also in stretto, in which the chromatic motif, now rising, is doubled between the bass and alto. We saw in the Prelude the critical role of the rising chromatic and its association with intense emotion. And, indeed, this passage does lead to an emotionally charged episode of triplets rushing from voice to voice, climaxing in bar 21—a climax intensified by the union of the triplet motif of the theme with its inversion.

The final moments of the Fugue are pensive and grave, with the music sinking in tonal depth, from which the theme surges in one last impassioned statement. Throughout the study of the D minor *WTC* pieces, we have seen Bach using specific musical language patterns in common within them and in other compositions in this tonality. I mentioned the motif in the theme of Sinfonia 4 being part of the subject of the Fugue in Book I. Both that Sinfonia and this Fugue in Book II close with descending chromatic harmony and a unison on the tonic.

FINAL TWO BARS of Sinfonia No. 4.

There is a deep affinity between the D minor compositions, not only between the Sinfonia and the *WTC* pieces but also and especially between those in the *WTC* and the *Art of the Fugue.*

Because so many themes and motifs in the D minor Preludes and Fugues are included in the composer's monumental and beloved last work, they too share with the latter profound sentiment and transcendental beauty.

7

E-Flat Major

Bach was inspired to write some of his most beautiful compositions in E-flat major. Not only did he often use it to symbolize the Trinity, but through its tonality he expressed the noblest of human affections—dignity, confidence, and serene happiness reflecting inner peace and harmony. We find them all in the Preludes and Fugues in this key in the WTC.

Among the relatively few instrumental compositions in E-flat major the following are of special note: Invention no. 5, Sinfonia no. 5, French Suite no. 4, Suite for unaccompanied cello BWV 1010, organ Prelude and Fugue BWV 552 (the St. Anne), organ Trio Sonata BWV 525, and Sonata for flute and clavier BWV 1031.

In the choral works the following numbers in this key, and perhaps the most familiar, are truly sublime: the contralto solo *Sehet, Jesus hat die Hand* (See, Jesus stretches out his hand) in the *St. Matthew Passion*; the bass arioso *Betrachte, meine Seel'* (Bethink thee, my soul) in the *St. John Passion*; and from Cantata 140, the first chorus *Wachet auf* (Sleepers, awake) and the fourth chorale *Zion hört die Wächter singen* (Zion hears the warders sing).

Prelude, E-Flat Major, Book I

In keeping with the symbol of the Trinity implied in the key signature, Bach designed this Prelude in three sections, a preamble, a chorale (in the form of a fugato) and a double fugue. That it is also the seventh key, that number being a holy symbol, must also have been a factor in his choosing an unusual and distinctive form for this Prelude.

The preamble has a distinct improvisatory character. One can easily imagine Bach responding to an improvisation request from a gathering of friends or an aristocrat and beginning in just this way.

Among the religious symbols found in Bach's music is one that is known as the Flight of Angels. Its identification is based on the Chorale Prelude *Vom Himmel kam der Engel Schar* (From heaven came a group of angels), the first of the canonic variations on the hymn *Vom Himmel hoch, da komm' ich her* (From high heaven come I here), and in several pictorial images in the cantatas. Melodies which rise and fall in a regular pattern are characteristic of this symbol. Such a pattern is evident throughout the preamble. It is with this symbolic image that Bach prepares for entry into the serene and exalted atmosphere of the chorale.

The distinguishing feature of the chorale melody is the rising interval of the perfect fourth, a fundamental religious symbol often associated with the Trinity. This interval is prominent in the chorale of the St. Anne Fugue, mentioned earlier.

Also of special interest, the four-note thematic melody of the chorale in this Prelude closely resembles the opening melody of the Passion Chorale.

The fugue begins with elegant simplicity and is built on the melodic themes of the preamble and chorale. Through Bach's inimitable creative imagination and skill, the effect of the union of these two themes is beatific.

Several other numeral symbolic references enrich our contemplation of this Prelude. The number three also occurs in multiple form. The preamble is nine bars in length and the chorale is 15 bars in length (a double symbolism here, for the number 5 is a symbol of the cross).

A variation of the chorale theme is introduced in the second bar of the fugue (bar 26) and its fourth entry is worthy of note. It occurs in bar 43, a number symbolic of the word credo (C-3, R-17, E-5, D-4, O-14 = 43) and is marked by a spectacular voice-crossing as the variation motif leaps a compound fourth to soar above the other voices.

Because numerical symbolism is deeply ingrained in Bach's design for this Prelude, it would not be surprising to find that he included a symbolic personal identification as well. We know that he did this often and with varying degrees of emphasis in many compositions, especially those of a spiritual nature. We are thinking here of the numbers 14 (Bach) and 41 (J. S.

Bach). At bar 41 there is a special cadence to C minor, the only one which is ornamented. Then when we look at the total length of the Prelude the number 70 is 14 times 5—his personal symbolic number combined with the symbolic cross number. Unobtrusive, yes, but it is there.

Now let's look at another facet of the character of this piece. You will no doubt have discovered how illusive the metrical pulse is when playing the chorale. The usual accents of quadruple time do not seem to work. Bach is following here the rules of Stile Antico, reminiscent of olden times such as Palestrina. It is a style where the music flows so that accents and nonaccents in the various voices do not coincide. When tension increases in one voice, it decreases in another. The effect is one of a continuous flow of independent melodic lines, as though there were no bar lines. This does not change in the fugue—the rules of the style continue and apply to the relationship of the Flight of Angels melodies with the chorale theme.

This is not an easy Prelude. It demands careful voice leading, meticulous finger control and, especially in the fugue, thoughtful planning with perceptive awareness of the effect of the harmonic modulations to develop and sustain expressive intensity through to the end. Yet even the process of mastering these difficulties brings its rewards. Every step toward perfection becomes a revelation as the beauty of the music slowly permeates the consciousness.

Meaningful as the symbolism is in contemplating Bach's creative genius, it is the glory of the sound of the music that ultimately affects us. Perhaps no one has expressed the essence of this Prelude more thoughtfully than Landowska when she wrote, "Its beauty lies in the never ending ebb and flow of waves which, from beginning to end, bestows upon the whole piece a calm grandeur, something eternal that goes beyond the last bars" (*Landowska on Music*, p. 185).

Fugue, E-Flat Major, Book I

In his comments on these two pieces, Spitta had reservations about the suitability of this Fugue as a companion to the Prelude. Whereas the Prelude "is most noble, deep, and purposeful," the Fugue, he felt, "notwithstanding its grace and sweetness, is too light when compared with the Prelude" (*J.S. Bach*). He thought the two pieces could not possibly have been designed at the same time. Even if Spitta is right about the chronology, we can be sure that Bach had definite reasons in the matter.

For one thing, would not a feeling of joy naturally follow such an exalted spiritual experience reflected in the Prelude? And would it not be most directly expressed through melodic and motivic material and captivating

harmony alone, without complicated fugal devices? The joyful character of
the Fugue, embodied in the subject and countersubject and especially in
the rhythm, is by no means frivolous, but truly jubilant—infectiously so.

Echoes of the Prelude subtly link the Fugue with its companion. When
we look closely at the first part of the subject we see within it the melodic
motif of the Chorale of the Prelude—twice, in fact.

And toward the end there is a veiled reference to the rising and falling
melodic scale motif of the preamble. Then a further connection—the
closing cadence of both pieces has a descending chromatic melody of C,
C-flat to B-flat. In the Fugue this is emphasized by its appearance in a fourth
voice.

As in the Prelude, here too numerical symbolism relating to the Trinity can be discerned in Bach's design. The number three is beautifully woven
into the structure, either as itself or in multiple. The most obvious is that
it is written in three voices. There are nine entries of the theme. The subject (Dux) appears three times, whereas the answer (Comes) appears six
times. There are six episodes of which the first three are distinguished by a
descending chromatic harmonic progression. The third is especially distinctive. It is extended to five bars (a double symbolism here, five being a cross
symbol) in which movingly effective descending chromatic harmony flows
through the broken chord progressions in the treble in a modulation to C
minor.

The moment when Bach makes the reference to the preamble melody
is significant. It is at the 33rd bar and leads to the final entry of the theme.
This ninth entry (a Comes) is unlike any of the others. The countersubject
is absent, and in its stead we hear a sequence of pairs of solid chords, the
first containing an altered note (flatted 6th) in the theme to form a striking
diminished seventh to dominant seventh cadence, the second leading to a
deceptive cadence. A glorious climax heralding the conclusion of the Fugue,
but not the deep feeling of joy its music inspired. Bach has ensured that it
will remain with you long after the final chord.

Prelude, E-Flat Major, Book II

In his writings about Bach's music, Bodky mentions that in the key of
E-flat major "we find ... some of the most wonderful demonstrations of
'peace of mind,'" and cites this Prelude among particular examples (*Inter-*

pretation of Bach's Keyboard Works). This is, I think, an apt description of the mood and tone of sentiment one senses throughout the music.

The opening bars contain two figures of special note. The bass melody begins with a mordent, which was prominent in the subject of the E-flat Fugue in the first book—a subtle connecting thread. Then the end of the mordent falls an octave as a four-note-form chord. An octave descent in a specific context has been identified as a Sanctus or holy symbol, as heard in the Sanctus of the *B minor Mass*. There are occasions with definite related connotations when Bach filled in this octave with notes of the chord. Two such examples are Recitative no. 28 in the *St. John Passion*, when Jesus says, *Du sagst's, ich bin ein König* ("Thou sayest, I am a king") and Recitative no. 18 in the *St. Matthew Passion*, when Jesus asks of his disciples in the garden of Gethsemane, *Setzet euch hie, bis dass ich dort hingehe und bete* ("Sit ye here, while I go yonder and pray").

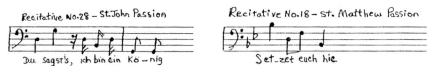

That this descending chord figure in the bass line has a Sanctus connotation would be very relevant in the Trinity key. The symbolism implied in its melodic figuration, and its significance in the structure of the composition, is underscored by its overt exposure. Bach planned that when it appears, nothing ever accompanies it. He also included numerical symbolism for this bass figure in his plan. In direct relation to the Trinity theme, established at the outset by the time signature—three groups of three—this Sanctus symbol occurs nine times.

Besides the mordent, there are two other elements in the composition that evolved from the two pieces in this key in the first book and, in a kind of alchemical process, take on a new dimension in expressive beauty. The first is the undulating character of the melodic phrases, suggesting, as it did in the preamble of the earlier Prelude, the Flight of Angels symbolism—a pictorial theme contributing a great deal to the ambient mood. The second is the series of chromatic progression heard in the earlier Fugue and here used in the development in the second part of the Prelude to build emotional tension. The effect of the chromaticism is considerably heightened by the bass line Bach chose to accompany it—melodic leaps in a gigue-like rhythm. Bach contrasts the two chromatic passages with opposing directional leaps in the bass. Falling sevenths are abruptly exchanged for rising ninths. A stroke of the master. Leaps of the ninth are often associated with distress, but here that symbolic tendency serves instead to create climactic thrust in a glorious moment of exaltation which apexes at bar 43—the symbolic number for the word *credo*. I noted in the earlier Prelude that Bach gave special treatment to this same bar.

Two additional figures, one which looks back and one which looks forward, and both with joyful overtones, are worth noting: the rhythmic motif ♫ ♩, heard at the end of the climax in the middle section, was an integral motif in the earlier Fugue and the turn, appearing twice here, will be important in the companion Fugue.

Beginning with the Sanctus theme, then leading through a sequential descending harmonic progression marked by a gigue-like rhythm in the bass to a climactic pause, with a jubilant cadenza Bach brings the Prelude to a close with a final Sanctus reference—formed in the first notes of the descending triplets and, most affirmatively, in the final bar. A consummate expression of the joy of inner serenity and cosmic grace.

Fugue, E-Flat Major, Book II

To conclude his group of pieces in this key Bach returns to the Stile Antico of the Prelude in the first book. Chorale, and therefore vocal, in style, Bach elicits from the tonal realm of E-flat major music of wondrous clarity and eloquence.

The musical language of this Fugue is firmly rooted in motivic ideas from the three preceding pieces, and symbolic references remain indigenous to the Trinity theme.

The subject consists of 15 notes, a number that correlates with the chorale in the first book, which is 15 bars in length and as noted then, encompasses both the number three of the Trinity and the number five, a cross symbol. Also in common with the earlier chorale the symbolic religious interval of the fourth and the four-note melody resembling the opening of the Passion Chorale are part of the melodic theme.

The mordent, which was brought forward from the Fugue in the first book as an important motif for the Prelude in the second book, is now given supreme status in this Fugue. Not only is it included in the theme but permeates the countersubject and all the episodes—appearing no fewer than 40 times. Its rhythm is another form of the joy motif heard in the preceding Prelude and the earlier Fugue—/♫ ♩ / ♫ ♩.

Returning to numerical symbolism of the Trinity theme, we can discern further reference to it in Bach's design. You will remember the turn we noted in the Prelude. Bach has brought it forward as part of the countersubject. But we can see he has assigned it a special role—to amplify the affect implied in the subject. He has given it a unique rhythm, incorporating another form of the joy motif (♫ ♩) and ensured that it be heard only three times (the third time double-voiced) and confined it exclusively to the exposition. Having established the spirit of jubilation amidst the Trinity symbolism, he now moves on to the next phase.

Bach does not display intricate contrapuntal devices in this Fugue, but now he uses the stretto to increase emotional fervor. And in this he has made another symbolic reference to the Trinity. There are precisely three stretti. The first two begin the middle section and build the music to the highest tonal level of the composition, and the third, between the soprano and the bass, ushers in that all-important, consummate final statement.

Wonderful things happen between the first two stretti and the third. The extended episode is striking in its beautiful dialogue between the voices. But five symbolic elements reveal a deeper dimension to this passage. All have a relationship to what came before, and inimitably Bach brings them all together in preparation for his glorious concluding statement. Let's begin with numerical symbolism. It is entirely in three voices and is 15 bars in length, this latter number, with its double symbolism, already represented in the subject theme. The next number is the one symbolic of the word credo—the number 43. That it was important to Bach as part of the Trinity theme is evident. This bar was singled out for special treatment in both Preludes in this key, and at this moment he begins this meaningful interlude. The fourth element also concerns this bar. In the bass melody we hear the drop of an octave, the first of three statements of the Sanctus symbol so important in the companion Prelude. The fifth element is of extraordinary import. The pictorial Flight of Angels melody from the preamble in the first Prelude appears now in the bass at bar 47 and is repeated three times. The stage is now set for the reentry of the subject (Dux). And a very special one indeed. Not only is it the ninth and combined with the Angels symbolism, but melodically begins with an interval of a fourth instead of a fifth and is in the key of A-flat—the only time it is heard in a key other than the tonic or dominant.

During this singular appearance of the theme, the soprano falls silent. Its reentry is momentous. Joined in stretto with the bass, this dramatic final statement of the theme, followed by the descent of the soprano through a sublime harmonic progression to the octave below, a cadence crowned with a signature melody in the tenor of a mordent and interval of the fourth, is a culmination of the spirit of joy and exaltation Bach has expressed throughout the four pieces.

That he felt a very personal relationship with the spirit embodied in the music he created in E-flat major for the WTC may have been intimated at the beginning and reiterated at the end. Both the first Prelude and this final Fugue in the set are 70 bars in length. This number, as we noted, is the multiple of 14, the symbol for Bach's name, and 5, a symbol of the cross.

8

E-Flat Minor/ D-Sharp Minor

PRELUDE Eb minor I

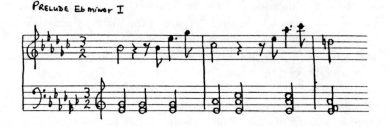

Fugue—D# minor—Bk.I

Prelude—D# minor—Bk.II

Bodky said that the Preludes and Fugues in E-flat minor/D-sharp minor are "gems for connoisseurs" (in particular those in Book II) (*Interpretation of Bach's Keyboard Works*). Bach did have this in mind when, in the subtitle to the Third Part of the *Clavier Übung*, he wrote, "For the enjoyment of the soul of connoisseurs [Kennern] and true amateurs [Liebhabern]." Of course, the whole of the WTC could be described in Bodky's words, but the four pieces in this tonality are indeed directed toward the discerning (and undaunted) keyboard player. Bach not only displays his supreme mastery of counterpoint for us to study closely and makes exceptional demands on the player, he also calls forth intense emotional response and revelation.

Prelude, E-Flat Minor, Book I

To set the mood for our study of this Prelude, I would like to begin by quoting a moving passage from Robert Craft's book *Stravinsky: Chronicle of a Friendship 1948–1971* (p. 411). [April 7] "His piano is [in New York] exactly as it was there, [in California] with the manuscript drawing board over the keys, and, on top, the portraits of Monteverdi, Mozart, Beethoven, and Bach, whose *Well-Tempered Clavier*, Book I, is still open to the Prelude in E-flat minor, which he had been playing on Saturday." (He died the following Tuesday, April 6, 1971.)

This Prelude is a dramatic, heart-rending depiction of acute, almost paralyzing grief, the pain invariably associated with sudden calamity and loss. The music reflects this most traumatic of life's experiences.

There are manifold sorrows and griefs, and many, if not all, are musically expressed by Bach somewhere within the 48 Preludes and Fugues. None, perhaps, has such personal connotations as this Prelude. The particular event, that in all likelihood relates to this composition, occurred in July 1720.

Having left his wife, Maria Barbara, in good health in Cöthen, Bach returned from a trip to Carlsbad with Prince Leopold to find that she had suddenly died and was already buried. This loss was compounded by the fact that he was left with four young children bereft of their mother. That Bach would choose to express this most devastating experience in E-flat minor is highly significant. It is also revealing that, of the four pieces in this tonality in the *WTC*, this is the only one in the flat key. All the others are in D-sharp minor (although transposed in many editions for easier reading). A singular emotional experience assigned to a singular key.

The whole melodic and harmonic design of the music portrays unprecedented anguish. The melody, vocal in style, bursts forth as a cry of despair. The articulation of these notes must capture the drama implicit in the jagged, angular intervals and abrupt melodic leaps.

In Cantata 124 *Meinen Jesum lass ich nicht*, the tenor aria *Und wenn der harte Todesschlag* (And when the cruel blow of death / Weakens the senses, touches the limbs), begins with an almost identical melody as this Prelude.

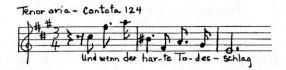

It is sung with great agitation in keeping with the text, a text easily transferred in one's mind to this music and a clear guide to interpretation. An important feature in the aria is a rhythmic motif ♪♫♫♪♪ ♪|♪♫♫♪♪ ♪, which has been described as the "blow of death" or a "terror" motif. It is played by the strings accompanying the solo. I always hear this motif when I play the Prelude.

The first section deals with the impact of the first moments in the tragedy, the mind stunned with overwhelming disbelief, the body numb from shock. Could the tearing leaps be anything other than pleading cries of "why? why?" These cries reach their apex when the melody reaches the highest note in the piece at bar 11 on that Baroque symbol of pain and terror, the diminished seventh chord.

What is also symbolically important is that this chord forms the main climax, exceptional by coming so early in the piece, yet exactly where the greatest emotional intensity would naturally occur. It is the crucial turning point when sobbing will subside into weeping after the modulation to B-flat minor.

The music will continue to go through several climaxes in the middle section. Waves of emotion move through the rhythmic agitation of the canonic melody with its drops of diminished fifths, to chords with the descending bass motif pulling the memory back to the first section, then with a sudden outburst sweeps upward to culminate on the stunning chord of the Neapolitan sixth at bar 26.

Bach follows this poignant moment with a passage of deeply moving pathos, the crest of which turns back on the symbolic interval of sorrow, the diminished third (an interval rarely found in Bach's melodies) and leads us to the tender and exquisite deceptive cadence at bar 29.

From here to the end, Spitta says, "the sentiment is as sad as death and the change to the major at the close awful" (*J.S. Bach*). Bach has, in this Prelude, portrayed the soul's tortured transition from despair to resignation with music unparalleled in beauty and eloquence.

> Can I see another's woe,
> And not be in sorrow too.
> Can I see another's grief,
> And not seek for kind relief.
> —William Blake

Fugue, D-Sharp Minor, Book I

As would be expected, Bach has followed the Prelude with a Fugue that has at its core material directly relevant in sentiment. The subject of 13 notes (which is also the length of the subject of the D-sharp minor Fugue in Book II) begins with a motif of profound symbolic meaning. A melodic progression which rises a fifth, moves to the minor sixth and returns to the fifth was an established pattern identified with sorrow and deepest despair. There are many instances in the choral works where Bach chose this motif for melodies in which grief and longing are communicated. Two examples are particularly meaningful.

In the opening chorus of Cantata 177, the first lines of the text are: *Ich ruf' zu dir, Herr Jesu Christ, / Ich bitt,' erhör mein Klagen, / Verleih mir Gnad' zu dieser Frist, / Lass mich doch nicht versagen* (I call to Thee, Lord Jesus Christ, / I beg Thee, hear my complaint; / Grant me grace at this time, / Let me not despair).

Then there is the hauntingly beautiful flute solo in the soprano aria (no. 49) *Aus Liebe will mein Heiland sterben* (For love will my Savior die) in the *St. Matthew Passion*.

The last section of the subject contains that fundamental religious symbol—the interval of the fourth, a thematic interval throughout the E-flat
minor and D-sharp minor Preludes and Fugues. The answer not only begins
with this important symbol but, even more significantly, begins with the
same three notes that began the Prelude.

The countersubjects, with their free-flowing melodies seem to have been
chosen for their gentle effect—balm for the soul after the tortured jagged
leaps in the Prelude. But always, there are intimations of sorrow—the
descending chromatic scales (bars 10–11, 63, 73–74); jarring dissonances in
bars 15, 38 and 81; and a clear echo of pain in the stabbing leap in the
soprano in bar 41. Ponder this last one a moment. The number 41 is the
numerical symbol which represents Bach's name (J-9, S-18, B-2, A-1, C-3,
H-8). Perhaps it is not a coincidence that this pointed reference to the Prelude is placed in this bar.

During the first section of the Fugue, Bach avoids any modulation to
a major key. At bar 17, where it seems he will go to F-sharp major, he deliberately turns away and prepares to move to A-sharp minor. This marks the
beginning of the second section.

We now enter a realm where the magnitude of Bach's genius astounds
us and deepens our musical experience on both an intellectual and an emotional level.

From bar 19 to 23 a stretto between the soprano and alto aches with
heightened pathos. Bach, as a variation, has placed a rest before the last four
notes of the theme, forming a motif (a sobbing gasp?) to which he gives special emphasis, particularly in the fourth repetition with its piercing high
pitch. After the cadence at bar 24, another stretto begins. This passage
becomes the turning point in the emotional crisis which Bach emphasizes
with the alto counterpoint in 1.5 times augmentation. Then, how gently
does the flowing bass melody release the tension, a release fully realized by
the modulation to the major key? It is here that Bach introduces the subject in its inversion.

This melody, now major in tonality, no longer has the grief motif, yet
the initial drop of the fourth is imbued with a melancholy of its own. (See
the opening of the F-sharp minor Prelude in Book II.) This seems to represent an emerging from the darkness. Rays of optimism appear on the hori-
zon. Perhaps this is ephemeral, for by the second entry of the inverted
theme, a minor tonality has crept in. At bar 44 a powerful climax is reached
with this theme booming out in the bass in its major form followed by a
spectacular entry in the soprano ringing out high above the other voices,
strong in its 1.5 times augmentation. At bar 52 a dramatic dialogue between
the two themes unfolds. A triple stretto of the subject followed by a triple
stretto of the inversion culminates with the soprano moving through the

symbolic interval of sorrow which we heard in the Prelude—the diminished third.

At bar 61 the last section begins with a climactic stretto in which the subject is heard this time in double augmentation in the bass. This heralds a conclusion to the Fugue of monumental proportions. Who cannot feel the anguish of the diminished third and the descending chromatic scales in the soprano melody in the last episode preceding the final entry of the subject? It is in this final entry, a magnificent stretto of the true subject with its two forms of augmentation, that we feel the full impact suffering has made on the soul. We can only marvel at Bach's incomparable mastery of counterpoint—the genius lies in the emotional power attained within the counterpoint laws.

As though to remind us of the cause of this grief, Bach follows this with a passage of descending triads, a reference to the melody of descending fifths in the middle section of the Prelude.

The soaring final passage with its chromaticism in the soprano, three repetitions of a motif from the subject in the other voices and a cadence on a major chord, is surely a phoenix rising from the ashes.

Prelude, D-Sharp Minor, Book II

In this beautiful two-part invention, which Landowska has described as a "cantilena veiled with melancholy" (*Landowska on Music*, p. 199), we shall see that Bach has carried forward into Book II the mood and sentiment of the pieces in this tonality in the first book—even to the extent of making motivic references to them.

The image of the rising phoenix in the final bars of the D-sharp minor Fugue in Book I is also seen in the melodic pattern of rising alternate thirds in the first section of the theme of this Prelude. What is of special significance is the falling octave, the Sanctus symbol (from the *B minor Mass*) which Bach has placed in the bass accompanying the opening statement of the theme. It is found in several pieces in *The Well-Tempered Clavier* and is often an important clue to the interpretation of the music in which it occurs. The purport of the placement of this holy symbol is strengthened by the appearance in the second part of the theme of the rising interval of the fourth—the established fundamental religious symbol and absolutely fundamental to the design of both the Prelude and the Fugue in this set. Not only is this interval part of the theme, but it is given added emphasis in the motif first heard in the soprano in bar 3. This motif appears nine times which is a multiple of three—in itself a symbolic number representing, for Bach, the Trinity.

Cantata 131 *Aus der Tiefe rufe ich* (Out of the depths I cry unto Thee) contains relevant motivic passages that illuminate our understanding of the Prelude. The theme of chorus no. 3 is that of waiting for guidance, and the aria which follows it emphasizes waiting and patience. In the last chorus we find melodic motifs which Bach uses here. For the text *Und er wird Israel erlösen aus allen seinen Sünden* (And He will redeem Israel out of all its sins) the choir sings a melody which rises in a pattern of successive fourths and ends with a short scale.

There is also a melodic motif that rises in chromatic steps, similar to that which is heard at the end of the Fugue in Book I. The whole chorus expresses the joy of being lifted from the depth of despair to compassionate forgiveness.

Here too, in this Prelude, the Sanctus symbol, the rising melodic pattern and the interval of the fourth may be understood as expressing a belief in deliverance from adversity and confidence in the ability to find inner strength and understanding.

That Bach intended to link the E-flat minor Prelude in Book I to this Prelude in the second book is evident in the leaping soprano melody in bar 2, and especially in the angular, anguished diminished seventh cry in bar 14—bar 14—what could be more personal and revealing than that this passage appears in the bar which numerically symbolizes Bach's name? Did we not find a similar melodic reference in the Prelude in Book I at bar 41, that other personal numerical symbol?

An interesting feature of many of the pieces in the keys found only in the *WTC* is the rocking rhythmic pattern of a broken chord. It is an important element in the C-sharp major Prelude Book II, the F-sharp major Prelude Book II, the B major Prelude Book II and the G-sharp minor Prelude Book II. Why Bach chose this pattern for so many of these unique keys is certainly food for thought. Depending on the spirit of each piece, this rhythmic figure creates a feeling of contentment, comfort or equilibrium. This last is perhaps the most fitting in this case. It is interesting, too, to see that

Bach has, in bar 20, combined this figure in the bass with a faltering syncopated rhythm in the soprano.

Last but not least in our contemplation of this Prelude is the inclusion of the beautiful melodies in 32nd notes. Landowska identified the motifs in the last two bars of the first and second sections as originating from a gavotte, a French *bergerette* of the eighteenth century. This bucolic reference with its closing melody symbolically rising to resolve on an upper appoggiatura is one of those magical touches that affect the interpreter and the listener at the deepest level and brings Bach very close to us.

Fugue, D-Sharp Minor, Book II

We come now to the great meditative and reflective Fugue which unifies Bach's whole communication in the tonality of E-flat minor/D-sharp minor.

The subject of 13 notes (as was that of the Fugue in Book I) is characterized by the symbolic interval of the fourth. The opening notes also contain a motif closely connected to Cantata 131, which played an important role in our contemplation of the Prelude. In the tenor aria the altos sing, in conjunction, a chorale whose melody echoes these opening notes and is, with the long sustained notes, symbolically indicative of waiting and patience.

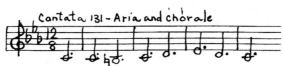

The countersubject motif subtly alludes to the theme of the companion Prelude, rising in consecutive thirds, but ornamented with passing notes.

Of particular interest in the design of this Fugue is the music of the episodes for Bach did not use material from either the subject or the countersubject. Instead, he created a new motif, singularly affecting and marked by intervals of the fourth.

The memory of the pain depicted by angular leaps in the Prelude in Book I surfaces here by several leaps of the octave. We cannot miss the poignancy of the soprano's sudden jump to the high A in bar 12. Another of equal significance is again in the soprano in bar 27. This dramatic leap precedes the 10th entry of the subject, which begins a passage of breathtaking harmonic progression in which the Neapolitan sixth is decisive in the emotional impact. At the end of this section, in the alto melody at bar 34, we hear again that rare interval that appeared, also at a specially chosen moment, in both the Prelude and the Fugue in Book I, the diminished third.

In the third episode the melancholy, which the soul has striven so hard to overcome, threatens to engulf the heart once more, but slowly it subsides in gently falling scale sequences and comes to rest in descending chromatic steps.

The 13th entry of the subject in the bass, which begins the final section of the Fugue, expresses a powerful resurgence of the spirit, resolute and confident in its declamation. Ushered in with a soaring soprano melody above it, then fortified by solid chords, the intervals of the fourth clearly ringing out under the rests, it is magnificent in its effect.

But this is not the last statement of the theme, for Bach chose to conclude the Fugue with a 14th entry. As we know, this numerical symbol for his name, wherever and in whatever form it appears, is always significant. Here, Bach has presented the subject in a very special way, for beneath it the answer, in inversion, appears in the tenor—in perfect mirror counterpoint. This passage, with its indelible personal signature and an increase of voices, forms one of the strongest and most affirmative conclusions in the whole of the collection.

Throughout this tonality, Bach has expressed, and shared with us, a most profound human experience.

9

E Major

PRELUDE E major I

FUGUE E major I

PRELUDE E major II

In the early Baroque period, E major was the Key of Heaven, since it was the sharpest and therefore "highest" key then in common use. Bach would certainly have been aware of this historical attribution. Its pure, crystalline timbre is reflected in all the instrumental works he wrote in this key. Serenity, charm, gracefulness, and vivaciousness are the dominant qualities in the music.

The repertoire is extensive and rich in variety. It includes Invention no. 6, Sinfonia no. 6, Prelude no. 5 of the *Six Little Preludes*, The sixth French Suite, a clavier concerto, a sonata for violin and clavier, a Partita for solo violin, a violin concerto, and an organ Toccata and Fugue.

Prelude, E Major, Book I

Bach originally wrote this Prelude in 1720 for Wilhelm Friedemann when the boy was nine years old. He did not change it in any way but transferred it directly to the *WTC*.

The Prelude, a Siciliano, is an exquisite depiction of a pastoral scene. A shepherd's flute echoes through the graceful melodies and delicate ornaments. The peaceful ambience suggests the gentle awakening of life in the meadows at dawn. There are flashes of emerging activity in the little rhythmic joy motif ♫ and the sudden flurry of 16th note turns at the beginning of the second half of the piece. But Bach has included a wistful mood, too, an aura of loneliness, reflected in the leap of the minor ninth, an interval associated with sorrow, and the descending chromatic scale—a mood gently checked by the little joy motif.

It is interesting to compare this Prelude with the Sinfonia and Invention in the same key, for Bach used similar motifs in all three pieces. In the theme of the Sinfonia there is a melodic motif that resembles part of the theme of the Prelude.

In both pieces he interjects just one moment of playful 16ths in the flow of triplets. Both pieces are so similar in mood and design that Bach must have felt a natural attraction to paint bucolic tone pictures in E major. The Invention starts with a descending chromatic scale, but it certainly doesn't have the same implication we hear in the Prelude. If anything, it's a sly, deceptive little motif (and syncopated to boot), for in fact, the music, bubbling with joy motifs (♫♩) is, as Spitta says "full of roguish fun" (J.S. Bach).

Bach's harmonic design for the Prelude is particularly affecting. Especially the beautiful modulation to F-sharp minor and, toward the end, the unexpected transitions through E minor and C major. All the elements in the music are colors in the tone painting. The plagal cadence that closes the piece is like a heavenly benediction.

Fugue, E Major, Book I

From the mystical atmosphere of dawn, the scene now shifts dramatically. The sun has fully risen, and life erupts in a frenzy of activity. A celebration of a new day. The air reverberates with the warbling of birds and playful antics of animals. The whole Fugue is filled with exuberant high spirits.

The opening motif, the rising step, actually appeared at the beginning of the Prelude in the first two notes of the tenor melody, and this motif will be the opening notes of both the Prelude and Fugue in E major in the second book. With this tiny motif, Bach the magician transports us to four different realms—all of them sublime.

Here, it is a call to begin a chase. The challenge is accepted and the game doesn't let up for a second. A profusion of racing scales and bounding leaps keeps the excitement at a feverish pitch, full of uninhibited gaiety and the sheer joy of being alive.

Among the leaps just mentioned, many are intervals of the sixth. Bach often wrote them into his melodies to express joy and happiness. He uses them here almost exclusively to accentuate an entry of the main theme.

The countersubject, the simplest of motifs imaginable, is utterly captivating. Its mischievous and carefree character embodies the whole spirit of the Fugue. Bach obviously loved it. The motif is in all but 5 of the 29 bars of the piece. The whole scenario revolves around this delightful little melody.

A new and vibrant rhythmic motif (♩.♪ ♪♩) in the bass is introduced just before a spectacular leap of a compound sixth heralds the final entry of the theme and the end of a glorious depiction of joy in nature. If you are in a particularly happy mood or perhaps your spirits need lifting, this is the Prelude and Fugue to play or listen to.

Prelude, E Major, Book II

From the pastoral ambience of the E major Prelude in Book I, Bach now lifts us to the pristine atmosphere of an alpine meadow at the height of flowering glory. This is a Prelude of ethereal beauty, sublime in its lucid texture and melodic and harmonic design.

We know that Bach was very fond of his first book of the WTC. It should not be surprising then if he referred to it while working on the second book and was inspired to relate the pieces in the same key in both books in subtle and ingenious ways. We see evidence of this throughout the collection.

This Prelude not only begins with the rising step motif which appears in both the Prelude and Fugue in the first book but the whole six-note opening melody is tonally identical to the tenor melody at the beginning of the Prelude in Book I.

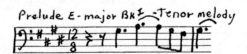

When we compare the step motif in the six-note theme of the Fugue in Book I with that of the six-note melody that begins this Prelude, we immediately feel the transformation Bach effects in the latter with a tied note and the turn which follows it. The music will evolve around this graceful and elegant ornament.

The turn may have had a special symbolic meaning for Bach when composing in the key of E major. He included it in the vibrant opening melody of the Preludio of Partita no. 3 for solo violin.

In Cantata 49, for the exceptionally beautiful duet *Dich hab' ich je und je geliebet* (I have loved thee for ever and ever) between the bass (Jesus, the

Bridegroom) and the soprano (the Soul, the Bride), Bach has written an organ accompaniment in which the turn, as the central figure, illuminates the joy and deep affection expressed in the words.

Special mention must be made of the rocking figure which appears near the end of both sections of the Prelude. Bodky calls this melodic octave pattern a "cradle symbol," citing in particular the passages where Bach wrote it in the accompaniment to the alto aria *Schlafe, mein Liebster* (Sleep, my Dearest) in the *Christmas Oratorio*. The mood that this figure symbolizes is what is relevant here—contentment and inner serenity, qualities so often associated with this tonality.

Bach seems to have had a special love for this Prelude. He made more small revisions to it than any other piece in the WTC, returning to it often in his last years. For instance, there are three versions of the bass in bar 50. The one that forms the turn seems the most fitting and may be the one he decided on.

Also, there are two versions of the final bar.

The last bars of the music may reveal why he chose the rich, full chord.

Bach could have ended the Prelude at bar 51, but instead he added a coda of spiritual dimensions, the music gently rising, lifting us to the celestial realm he will take us to in the companion Fugue.

This is a Prelude to treasure and come back to again and again.

Fugue, E Major, Book II

If we continue the analogy of ascending from a pastoral setting in the E major pieces in Book I to the higher elevation of an alpine meadow in the Prelude in Book II, then we are now standing on the summit of the mountain. Landowska describes this Fugue as of "incomparable magnificence" and "one of the most perfect works in music" (*Landowska on Music*, p. 200). It is a work of great spiritual intensity and power.

In this composition Bach is looking back to the music of the past. The spirit of Palestrina, whom Bach greatly admired and whose works he is known to have copied for close study, lives throughout this masterpiece.

The Fugue is written in the Stile Antico, traditionally associated with liturgical works of the Renaissance and characterized as vocal in style, marked by long note values and a slow tempo flowing without any strong rhythmic accents. Bach originally wrote 2/1 as the key signature, indicating the whole note as the rhythmic pulse.

One of the greatest of Bach's compositions, written also in Stile Antico, is the Credo in the *B minor Mass*. This, too, has the whole note as the metric pulse. A deep, significant relationship exists between that mighty chorus and this Fugue, not only in the style but in numerical symbolism. The number 43 symbolically represents the word *credo*. This is the sum of the alphabetical position of the letters: C-3, R-17, E-5, D-4, O-14. The Credo in the mass is 43 bars in length. This Fugue is 43 bars in length. The strength and confidence of the Creed so powerfully expressed in the chorus is our guide in interpreting the Fugue.

The subject opens with the rising step motif that began the themes of all the other *WTC* E major pieces. It is enlightening at this point to see the four themes side by side and to realize the transformation of affect Bach creates with this motif through rhythmic and melodic changes. All represent entry into four different realms of emotional experience.

The theme Bach chose for this Fugue is not in itself an imposing one, yet there is solemnity and dignity in its simplicity. It is precisely through this simplicity that Bach's creative imagination and contrapuntal skill excels.

The melody appears in several variations, including augmentation, diminution and inversion, and there are marvelous stretti, not only of the original
form but also in combination with the inversion and the augmentation and
diminution forms.

There are only two other instances where Bach used this theme, both
interesting in our overall contemplation. One is the chorale *Hilf deinem Volk,
Herr Jesu Christ* (Help Thy people, Lord Jesus Christ), the final prayer in the
great Cantata BWV119 *Preise, Jerusalem, den Herrn* (Praise, Jerusalem, the
Lord). It is a plainly set chorale, but what is particularly lovely (and unusual)
is the Palestrina-like flowing melody with which Bach adorns the word
Amen.

The other is found in the Canon Triplex À 6 Voc. This is the composition
Bach presented to the Society of the Musical Sciences on becoming a mem-
ber in 1747. It is the second of the three canons and can be clearly seen on
the paper Bach holds in the famous Haussmann portrait.

The exalted tone of the Fugue is magnified by the countersubject. The
melody with its firm ascending steps leading to the figure of the interval of
the fourth is a testimony of strength and affirmation. Palestrina wrote
this same figure for the second soprano in the Sanctus of his *Missa Papae
Marcelli.*

The interval of the fourth is especially meaningful, for it was historically a fundamental religious symbol linked to the Trinity. It is heard throughout the piece and given prominence in the final section beginning at bar 39. The countersubject, like the subject, appears in augmentation, diminution, and stretti.

Nothing conveys or builds emotional dynamics in music more powerfully than harmonic modulation. Bach was a master of this technique, and mean temperament opened up to him unlimited possibilities, even to the extent of defying the conventions of the time. His approach to the climax of the Fugue is a case in point. He intensifies the spiritual fervor to an extraordinary degree with a brilliant stretto of the original and diminution forms as well as the inversion of the theme while modulating to the most distant key in diatonic terms from the tonic. It is during this progression to G-sharp minor that the climax peaks on the unprepared chord of the ninth (bar 33). This was a daring move, for the chord of the ninth was considered at that time (and in the classical period as well) to be very harsh and dissonant. Also significant is the alto melody, which at the chord of the ninth has moved through a diminished third (A to F-double-sharp), an interval Bach used only at particularly tense moments.

Abruptly returning to the tonic key, Bach begins the coda with a magnificent stretto of the answer, subject, inverted diminished theme and countersubject. This is a pivotal moment. Now the fervent spirit of the Credo will reach celestial heights, climaxing with the rapturous soprano statement of the theme, its soaring melody reverberating as though in a cathedral setting—the ultimate homage to Palestrina.

Subject, countersubject, reiteration of the interval of the fourth, and the rising steps of the inversion of the theme all combine to bring this great Fugue to a glorious conclusion.

10

E Minor

Although often defined as the Passion key by its association with this theme in choral works, E minor proved to be a tonality Bach chose for a wide range of compositions, many of them among his most magnificent. It was also a tonality through which he created emotional dimensions of striking contrast in language of distinct character. These range from intense sorrow and suffering, to reflective serenity and contentment, to overt aggressiveness and adamant assertion. Such contrasts are evident in the Preludes and Fugues in both books in the WTC.

Most notable among the instrumental works are: Invention no. 7, Sinfonia no. 7, Partita no. 6, English Suite no. 5, Toccata no. 7, Sonata for flute and continuo BWV 1034, Sonata for violin and continuo BWV 1023, organ Trio Sonata BWV 528, and organ Prelude and Fugue (the "Wedge") BWV 548.

Among the choral works, two supreme examples are the opening chorus and the Duo e Coro (no. 33) *So ist mein Jesus nun gefangen* (So my Jesus now is taken) in the *St. Matthew Passion*. In direct relationship to this theme is Cantata 4, *Christ lag in Todesbanden* (Christ lay in the bonds of death), in which all seven sections are in E minor. Two arias in this key illustrate other themes of particular interest. They are the soprano solos *Lasst der Spötter Zungen schmähen* (Leave to mocking tongues their scorning) in Cantata 70 and *Ich bin vergnügt mit meinem Glücke* (I am content with my good luck) in Cantata 84.

Prelude, E Minor, Book I

A version of this Prelude appears in the *Clavierbüchlein* composed for Wilhelm Friedemann. In it, the figurative bass is accompanied only by solid chords indicating the harmonic progression. From a pedagogical aspect, this may have been a study in possible forms of the broken chord and in harmony. However, considering the technical level of the other Preludes in his son's book, surely there was more to it than that. It may well have been an assignment for Friedemann to begin to develop the skill of improvising a melody from the harmonic guidelines. We know he was a very gifted boy, and we can be sure the art of improvisation was part of his father's instruction. Friedemann was noted for his improvisations in later years.

Bach's version of the Prelude for the *WTC* is an eloquent realization with improvisational overtones based on the outline for Friedemann. He then added a new section, advancing the level of skill and dramatic import. The entire Prelude is constructed on one melodic figure which runs uninterrupted throughout—a remarkable demonstration of Bach's ingenious skill.

This improvisational section is as though scored for solo violin or flute, and cello with a lute providing harmony on every first and third beats. The short duration of these two-note chords ensures a distinct role as accompaniment to the melody. Some artists roll these two-note chords to give a lute effect.

With its hypnotic pulse, like waves of the sea constantly flowing and receding, the bass figure exerts a powerful influence on the cumulative affect created during the course of the melody.

The choice of tempi for this Prelude is a crucial decision. Important factors in both the first section and the Presto should be considered for optimum effect of the piece as a whole. The tempo of the first section is governed by the melody. Keller believed that "Bach conceived the key of E minor as masculine and powerful" (*The Well-Tempered Clavier*). It is certainly a concept to keep in mind. An undercurrent of passionate intensity drives this melody, and a tempo that realizes the full potential of the expressive implications of the various melodic figures is paramount. One of the implications, allied with the improvisational aspect, involves a discreet use of rubato, which does not disturb the flow of the music but heightens the emotional dynamic. We can discern here a foreshadowing of the Romantic era and the concept of a rubato melody over a steadily pulsating bass accompaniment. Note particularly Chopin's Prelude in E minor, Op. 28 no. 4.

A principal melodic figure in many of Bach's E minor compositions is the turn. Not only is it central to this Prelude, and its companion Fugue, and the Fugue in Book II, but also to the Sinfonia no. 7, the Allemanda in the sixth Partita, and the Organ Prelude BWV 548, in all instances appearing at or near the beginning.

What is astonishing is the myriad of tonal colors and emotional ambiences Bach creates using this simple ornament.

From its mood-setting initial appearance through to the final cadence before the Presto, the turn is fundamental in the melodic and harmonic development of the first part of the Prelude. We hear it in a variety of rhythmic forms and twice in the approach to each *point d'arrêt* in bars 10 and 12 at the critical dynamic modulations to E minor and C major. The momentum now builds through other melodic figures to the climax at bar 19 where the melody soars to its highest tonal level in the Prelude, after which the turn prepares the trill for the tonic cadence. The next two modulatory bars are a vital passage to the volcanic transition. They prepare for the Presto to begin in A minor, the key associated with dynamic energy and virtuosity in many of Bach's compositions. Regarding the tempo for this Presto, focus on dynamic energy. There is more to virtuosity than excessive speed.

The wave-like bass figure is now transformed into a raging storm. Above it the treble responds with parallel and opposing figurations, punctuated with dynamic leaps and scale passages. Two sequential turns propel the first leap in bar 24, and a single turn prepares a leap of a minor seventh in bar 33 to start the powerful descending harmonic progression from which an ascending scale catapults the music to the climax. Two whirlwind descending scales extend the tempestuous mood right through to the final cadence. The appearance of these descending scales at this point is portentous. Bach carries them forward to the Fugue with decisive intent.

The composer has not written a fermata over the final chord. By going immediately to the Fugue, maintaining the same tempo and focusing on dynamic energy, it will be clear from the character of the subject that the affect of the Fugue directly evolves from that of the Presto.

Fugue, E Minor, Book I

This Fugue, the only one in the *WTC* in two voices, is more in the canonic style of an invention than a conventional fugue. But it does have a countersubject and episodes. Its character is clearly defined by the two voices and forcefully imprinted by their interaction.

The design is straightforward, without any complex contrapuntal devices. It is divided into two sections, the second, beginning at bar 20, a transposed version with minor alterations of the first.

Most significant is the musical language Bach uses as the core of the affect. We find here three melodic figures that have a definite association with the key of E minor. The first is the rising four-note broken chord which begins the subject. The dramatic implication of beginning with this figure is evident in the Toccata of the sixth Partita, and, most notably, as the opening notes of the sopranos in the first chorus of the *St. Matthew Passion*. Bach extends its important role to episodes 2 and 4.

The second, which defines the very essence of the affect of the Fugue, is the descending chromaticism in the theme. Again, two examples from other works in this key show Bach using this chromaticism as a medium to project the principal character. These are the organ Fugue BWV 548 (The Wedge) and the Gigue of the fifth English Suite.

The third is the turn, already established in the Prelude and other cited compositions. Bach has brought it forward, incorporating it in the last part of the countersubject and in episodes 1 and 3.

From the turbulence of the Presto has risen a tone of confrontation, even pugnacity, liberally spiced with a healthy dose of humor. Characteristics amply displayed by the composer himself when circumstances merited them.

Establishing the mood with a bold, angular theme, Bach then heightens its dimension by bringing forward two key elements from the Presto—

leaps and descending scales, using them to the ultimate degree to amplify the affect.

Of the former, leaps of the sixth predominate, and, as Schweitzer (J.S. Bach) pointed out, when Bach used a lot of them in a piece they generally expressed joy. In this case, exhilaration probably best defines their symbolic intent. There are 28 pointed leaps of the sixth—a number symbolic in itself—for it is a multiple of 14, the number which represents B A C H (2 + 1 + 3 + 8 = 14), a secret code often found in his works to imply a personal identification with the spirit of the music.

Of the latter, these scales rant and rave, alone against opposing counterpoint, in parallel 6ths, 10ths, 13ths, and most belligerently of all, in defiance of the Baroque rules of harmony, in parallel octaves. Not once but twice, if you please, and at very strategic moments. Glenn Gould disliked any of Bach's octave passages, called it a "pedestrian device." Spitta commented on their "aggressive character" (J.S. Bach), but Keller divined their purpose as "a gathering of forces before the beginning of the second part and before the coda" (The Well-Tempered Clavier, p. 82). A rare occurrence certainly, but Bach did write them in a few other compositions.

The stalwart spirit of the chromatic theme is firmly imprinted on the finale, and the Fugue closes with a pointedly abrupt rolled tonic chord.

Prelude, E Minor, Book II

Having chosen to write the E minor Fugue in the first book in two voices, Bach then decided that the Prelude in this key in the second book also be in two voices. Following the early sonata form, it is binary with repeats.

A point of particular interest is the descending octave with which the piece begins. That it is worth noting lies in the fact that Bach began several pieces in this key with this figure. The Allemande and Courante in English Suite no. 5, Invention no. 7, Sinfonia no. 7, the Prelude BWV 938, the organ Prelude BWV 548 (The Wedge) and the organ Chorale Prelude BWV 646 all begin with a falling octave in the bass.

The important factor is its accentuation, prominently separated from the ensuing melodic phrase. As such, it has been established as a Sanctus symbol, from that chorus in the *B minor Mass*. But rather than being strictly confined to this symbolic interpretation, other dimensions may emanate from this sentiment. It may well be just an affirmation of the key, but this in itself is meaningful in that it places an emphasis on its tonality and its bearing on the affect created by the melodic material.

The essence of the mood underlying this Prelude may relate to the Chorale Prelude BWV 646 (mentioned above), which is based on the hymn *Wo soll ich fliehen hin* (Whither shall I flee). Indeed, the opening theme of this *WTC* Prelude, like the melodies in the Chorale Prelude, evokes a sense of anxious uncertainty with its twisting and turning and two entreating upward leaps—the latter melodic figure clearly defined in the questioning responses by the second chorus in passages in the first chorus of the *St . Matthew Passion* and much later by Schumann in his *Warum* (Why) in the *Fantasiestücke* Op. 12.

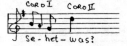

This restlessness and angst permeates the whole design of the Prelude with the running melodic figure appearing throughout, transposed, elaborated, inverted, in imitation, and even stretto (bars 24–28), many upward leaps, and fugitive harmonic progressions (note the move through six keys in bars 23–28).

In his design, Bach has brought forward from the two other E minor pieces in the first book two other elements besides melodic leaps. Many scale passages run in parallel motion and, again, we find the turn, this time not written out as part of a melody but indicated by the ornament symbol ᴕ. Some artists bring further emphasis to the turn by including it in the eighth note passages in bars 57–63, guided by its clear indication in a similar melodic figure in bar 78. This adds considerably to the pervading feeling of uncertainty.

Moving constantly between the theme and its inversion, pitting them against each other in bar 99, then presenting the theme in parallel 10ths in bar 103, the music finally comes to rest on a unison. But it does not pause before the Fugue begins. The transition will be electric.

Fugue, E Minor, Book II

The most striking feature about the fugues in this key in the WTC is their similarity in mood. Both are combative, even vehement. But, in contrast to the first Fugue, in this one Bach goes to considerable length to expand the dimension of this mood. As the Fugue develops we can also sense a quality of determination, in effect a direct response to the uncertainty evoked in the companion Prelude. By the time the piece reaches the final section, we realize a process of transformation has been taking place. The finale glows with confidence and certitude.

In rhetorical overtones, Bach immediately establishes the affect of the Fugue with a subject definitive in melodic and rhythmic figurations and specifically indicated marcato notes. For this theme Bach used three melodic figures from the previous pieces in this key, thus implying an evolutionary progression of affect that will reach its conclusion in this last piece. They are the turn, a rising tonal melody, and leaps. Another noteworthy observation about the theme is that it consists of 42 notes, a multiple of the number 14, the symbol for his name. A multiple of this number was also detected in the E minor Fugue in Book I. Awareness of this intimation of a personal identification with the mood of both pieces cannot help but affect our response to the music.

Having established a connection with the preceding pieces with three motivic references in the subject, Bach brings forward yet another in the first episode. It is the rising four-note-form chord from the subject of the

Fugue in Book I, now, in a different context, entirely transformed in character. The context lies in the role of the episode which seeks to mollify the aggressive tone of the exposition. And nothing contributes more to this alteration than the lilting rhythm Bach gives this broken chord as it sequentially leads the harmonic progression toward the entry of the subject in the bright and positive key of G major.

The countersubject is no less imposing than the subject. It too contains a rising melodic figure, and like the one in the subject is no longer "questioning" but assertive. This quality is affirmed by the strong measured steps of the half- and quarter-note melody leading to the cadence.

In contrast to the subject that remains constant without any complex devices such as inversion or stretti, it is the countersubject which is the focus of the contrapuntal treatment and goes through a series of transformations. During this process the theme is passed from one voice to another in what becomes a virtuosic display of cross-voicing, often melodically modified. Two striking modifications are prepared at significant moments. One is at bar 41, another numerical symbol for Bach's name (J S BACH—9 + 18 + 14 = 41). The other, at bar 71 in which the third voice takes no part , accentuates with dynamic leaps the ninth and final entry of the subject at its lowest and most resonant position.

There is, however, one appearance of the countersubject where placement and form take on symbolic dimensions. It is in the seventh entry of the subject (and at bar 49, a multiple of 7), a number sacred since ancient times, not only in biblical terms but in alchemical theory the gateway from Earth to heaven. It is here that Bach, for the only time after the exposition, presents the countersubject in its original form (slightly altered at the cadence) and, distinct from the six other appearances, is devoted entirely to one voice.

It is from this point that the emotional tidal flow slowly builds momentum in preparation for the great final entry of the subject. Numerical symbolism surrounds this powerful entry, for it is the ninth, a multiple of three, the most sacred number since the time of Pythagoras—a symbol of strength, justice, wisdom and peace, which Bach underscores with three stunning leaps in the countersubject.

As he has done in other pieces (e.g., the A-flat major Fugue in Book II), to create a particularly dramatic approach to the final statement Bach thinks in terms of the mighty sound of the organ to heighten the impact of the climax. Here, pedal-like bass figures augment the upward thrust of the soprano as it reaches the climax in bar 81 and add to the brilliance of the cadenza before the glorious conclusion. A passage indelibly imprinted by a rhythmic joy motif ♪♫♩, mordent, increase of voices, and most significantly, the Sanctus drop of the octave, the motif which began the Fugue's companion Prelude, on the major final chord.

11

F Major

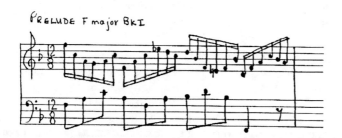

PRELUDE F major Bk I

FUGUE F major Bk. I

PRELUDE F major Bk. II

Bach's instrumental compositions in F major can be described as grand, majestic, vivacious and thrilling. They all demand considerable technical skill. Certainly, many works in this performance key have a special place in the repertoire of some virtuosi. The great trumpeter Adolph (Bud) Herseth has stated unequivocally that the Brandenburg Concerto no. 2 in F is the most difficult in all the repertoire for this instrument (Furlong, *Season with Solti*). For those privileged to hear him perform it, it will undoubtedly be an unforgettable experience.

Besides the two Brandenburg Concertos in F major, the Italian Concerto and the mighty Toccata and Fugue for organ are superb concert pieces. We must also include the fourth English Suite with its imposing Prelude. Duetto II, Invention 8, Sinfonia 8 and Preludes 8 and 9 from the *Twelve Little Preludes* all test the mettle of students. Bach did not even spare novices. The two little F major pieces in the *Anna Magdalena Notebook* are full of tricky rhythm patterns and ornaments. We expect no less from the Preludes and Fugues.

Speed is not necessarily a factor, but finger dexterity, an unerring sense of rhythm energizing the music with vitality, and command of the instrument certainly are. In the end though, it is the glory of the music that counts. Virtuosity is never an end in itself with Bach.

Prelude, F Major, Book I

To someone who complained that a supposedly easy piece was still too difficult, Bach replied, "Only practice it diligently, it will go very well; you have five just as healthy fingers on each hand as I" (David and Mendel, *The Bach Reader*, p. 352). I think there may have been a twinkle in his eye when he said this, and his tone encouraging.

C. P. E. Bach wrote that "Trills are the most difficult embellishments and not all performers are successful with them. They must be practiced industriously from the start" (*Essay*, p. 101). Could there be a more golden opportunity to develop and master this skill than in this Prelude? Of the many instances in his music where Bach indicates ascending and descending trills (sometimes played here with suffixes), it is here that they are most brilliantly displayed in all their glory.

With vibrant triplets in the bass leading the rhythm, spirited 16th notes and sparkling ornaments, the music dances and joviality pours from every bar.

Fugue, F Major, Book I

With the last notes of the Prelude ending abruptly on a weak beat, its companion Fugue begins almost on the next breath.

The subject is in the character of a Passepied, robust, earthy, and full of high spirits. Bach played through all of Book I three times for his pupil Heinrich Nicolaus Gerber (what lessons those must have been). How do you think he articulated the first five notes of this subject? Do you think he played them the same way at each of these "lessons"? Three professional interpretations are: (a) ♩♪♩ ♩ ♪♩ ; (b) ♪|♩♩♩|♩ ; (c) ♩|♩♩♩|♩ . All are musical, but the third is less convincing. Bach would most certainly have established the dance right off. Interestingly, the same five-note melody pattern, with similar articulation, is found within the theme of the lively Sinfonia in the same key.

Within the Fugue are three stretti weaving the "dancers" through close-knit patterns and there are many finger gymnastics including 4 3 4 3 on scale passages (reminiscent of the scale fingerings marked by Bach for Wilhelm Friedemann in the Applicatio which accompanied the table of ornaments).

There are many compositions in which Bach specifically identified himself. He used two symbolic devices to do this. One was to use the letters of his name to form a melodic motif—B (B-flat), A, C, H (B-natural). A notable example is in the *Art of the Fugue* where, in the last fugue (Contrapunctus 18), the third subject opens with these notes.

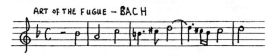

The other, which we find in this Fugue, was to represent his name by number symbolism—each letter having the value of its position in the alphabet (B-flat 2, A 1,C 3, B-natural [H] 8). When added together the magic number is 14. For a more emphatic purpose he would include the letters J-9 (J and I were considered the same letter) and S-18, thus signified by the number 41.

Here, the number 14 is significant. There are 14 subject entries in this Fugue with the 14th entry being special in that it is embellished with added notes.

Bach is not sitting on the sidelines watching this rustic dance. He's right in the middle of all the gaiety and loving every minute of it. And so should we.

Prelude, F Major, Book II

Similar to the C major Prelude in Book II, this Prelude, in five voices, is a supreme example of Bach's visionary conception of the broken chord. Once we have mastered the technical problem of finger control on sustained notes, we are free to become immersed in the music of this remarkable composition.

Resembling the texture and style of the great organ works, the harmony unfolds as each main note of a chord is sustained in succession while the melody flows from voice to voice in undulating waves of sound. Although this Prelude was created for a more intimate ambience, the cumulative effect of its rich sonorities is not unlike what one would experience in a cathedral. The turn, as integral here as it is in the C major Prelude, is the element in this graceful melody that gives it its unique charm. There is a sequential melodic pattern based on the turn in bars 41–46. This passage will occur in the Fugue—one of Bach's subtle links between a Prelude and its companion Fugue.

This is, perhaps, a Chorale Prelude in disguise. So often Bach's harmonization of a chorale contains a smaller rhythmic basis (the ♪ or ♪) which flows in perpetual motion amidst the sustained notes of the hymn, and a characteristic frequently found in the Chorale Preludes. The juxtaposition of broken chords, here embellished with passing notes which form two main melodic motifs, and solid chords creates constant surges of emotional tension.

Bach was passionately interested in discovering the hidden secrets of harmony, which he believed revealed transcendental wisdom. Indeed, throughout his music the power of his harmonic progressions amaze and enthrall us. It is well worthwhile to ponder deeply the harmonic journey Bach takes through this Prelude.

Notice particularly bars 53–56, where Bach pointedly exploits the value of mean temperament, moving from flats to sharps in a stunning transition at bar 53, daring and surely guaranteed to shock the "old guard." It became a technique dear to the heart of Schubert 75 years later.

From this climactic moment Bach brings us back to Earth, abruptly returning to F major and the main theme. In a beautiful harmonic progression rising through G minor to the final emotional apex in B-flat major, he leads us to the tranquil and serene conclusion.

Fugue, F Major, Book II

From the lofty realm of the Prelude, Bach comes truly down to Earth in this Fugue. It is a real, undisguised gigue, bubbling with humor.

That there is an affinity between the C major set in Book II and this pair in F major may indeed be a conscious design of the composer's. Is it not significant that both the beginning pieces and those that come at the end of the first half have Preludes of cosmic dimensions and Fugues of unmistakable mirth? We saw that the turn was a component in the melodies of both Preludes, and now we notice that both Fugues begin with the mordent.

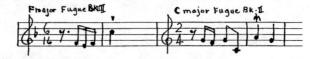

With the F major pieces, Bach marks a milestone in this treasury.

Bach has placed strokes on the strong-beat skips—a clear indication that the dance is of an especially energetic nature, for the stroke implies not only that a note is detached but also marcato. This energy is punctuated by two great leaps in the bass, up an 11th in bars 28–29 and down a 12th at bars 82–83. Bach tempers this boisterous activity with two gentle sequential passages. The first, from bars 38–44, is a direct transference of the melodic sequence in bars 41–46 of the Prelude.

The second, from bars 61–65, with its descending melodic motif over a pedal note, is a quiet moment when the dancers catch their breath. From this point the whole action regains momentum.

It is not difficult to imagine a real scenario for this Fugue. Let's take the Peasant Cantata as our starting point. This work was performed on 30 August 1742, in homage to the Chamberlain Karl Heinrich von Dieskau, who on entering possession of land, received a new title—Herr von Kleinzschocher. The peasants of the village gather to congratulate him and at the end, head for the tavern and free beer. There are 24 numbers (nearly all dance tunes) in this Cantata and, of special interest here, the last one is the only one in F major. The singers tell us they are going to the tavern where the bagpipe drones, happily shouting, "Long live Dieskau and his house, may he receive what he desires."

To bring this whole scene even more vividly alive in our imagination, the great painting "The Wedding Dance" by Pieter Bruegel the Elder, painted in 1566, depicts the very essence of this Fugue. Everything is there— even the bagpipes. The Fugue captures all the wonderful, uninhibited merry-making.

Bach, a Thuringian peasant himself, knows exactly how to bring this spectacular dance to a close. The penultimate subject entry in the soprano throws all caution to the wind. Foot-stomping chords bring in extra voices for the first two motifs and land, totally unexpected, on B-flat minor.

Excitement now reaches an all-time high as the bass, playing a few tricks with the theme, and booming the final statement under a whirlwind of 32nd notes, brings the party to a tumultuous close.

12

F Minor

Bach assigned a special role to the key of F minor. Through it he expressed the deepest sorrow, grief and longing, at times reaching tragic proportions. It is the music of a contemplative soul, never self-pitying or disillusioned, but profoundly probing the universal problems of life and death. It is Bach communicating on a most intimate and compassionate level.

When one considers Bach's vast output, the instrumental compositions in this key, including those in the WTC, form a small but very select group: Invention 9, Sinfonia 9, a clavier concerto, a sonata for violin and clavier, the organ Prelude and Fugue BWV534, and the organ Chorale Prelude BWV 639 *Ich ruf' zu dir, Herr Jesu Christ* (I cry to thee, Lord Jesus Christ).

Nothing conveys more definitively the emotional dimensions which, to Bach, were intrinsic to the key of F minor than the music he wrote in this tonality for his choral works. Three most moving numbers are the opening Sinfonia and chorus of Cantata 12 *Weinen, Klagen, Sorgen, Zagen* (Weeping, lamenting, worries, fears), the soprano aria *Zerfliesse, mein Herze, in Fluten der Zähren* (Release, oh my heart, thy torrents of weeping) in the *St. John Passion*, and the tenor aria and chorus *O Schmerz! Hier zittert das gequälte Herz* (Here trembles the troubled heart) in the *St. Matthew Passion*. The sorrow Bach expressed in his F minor choral works lies deeply ingrained in all his instrumental pieces in the same key.

Prelude, F Minor, Book I

Deep, pensive melancholy pervades this Prelude. Of special interest is the fact that both this piece and the Prelude in E-flat minor were included in the Clavierbüchlein for Friedemann, works of tragic implications yet evidently well within the emotional grasp of the nine-year-old boy. These pieces were written not long after and may relate to the death of Maria Barbara—a devastating experience for both father and son.

The undulating, never ceasing 16th-note melodies woven among the solemn long note melodies create an affect in close affinity with the Chorale Prelude *Ich ruf' zu dir.*

Chorale Prelude – Ich ruf' zu dir

The ponderous steps of the alto and tenor melody with which the piece begins has a counterpart in the theme of the organ Fugue in this key, a work that Schweitzer describes as "tremendously tragic precisely because (it has) divested itself of every shred of passion and expresses only great sorrow and deep longing" (*J.S. Bach*).

Bach exploits to the fullest degree the broken chord, enriching the resonance with sustained notes, a device which, in such a slow tempo, augments the effect of the beautiful harmonic modulations and transitions. Along with the broken chord there is an important little motif that is introduced in the second beat of the first bar and is heard throughout the Prelude.

It appears, with some intervalic variation, 30 times in the 22 bars of the piece. A little motif that somehow seems always searching, questioning.

The poignancy of the melody in bar 15 takes on an added dimension when we realize that the number 15 has symbolic implications. It is a multiple of five, a number which in Bach's music represents the five wounds inflicted on Jesus on the cross. The syncopated steps of the melody at the end of the bar are also symbolically significant. Bach, in his choral works, often depicted weariness and inner uncertainty in this way.

From this passage Bach leads us now to the closing section of the Prelude. By returning to the opening theme through an unexpected deceptive cadence, he forms a motif in the bass of bars 16–17 that will become the opening notes of the Fugue to follow.

After the reiteration of the opening theme the music flows and swells to the climax, its anguish and pathos increased with the alto's and tenor's ponderous steps now in double thirds above the pedal point, and the soprano's falling diminished sevenths, a long-established symbol of pain. How gently this climax subsides, but not without further diminished seventh harmony and one last symbol of deep distress—the falling dissonant ninth in the bass. Yet is there not a feeling of resignation in the final cadence?

Fugue, F Minor, Book I

Bach now follows the Prelude with a Fugue that continues but pene-
trates more deeply the theme of sorrow and anguish. Austere and noble, it
is one of the great spiritual compositions in the collection. The affect of the
piece is revealed in every note of the subject. Rarely do we find an almost
entirely chromatic subject melody in the WTC.

A melodic progression from the fifth to the minor sixth and back to
the fifth always held connotations of pain and deepest despair. Although
we do not hear a rise from the tonic to the fifth in the opening notes, the
essence of the plaintive melody is captured immediately. The next four notes
of the theme form a visually significant symbol. When a line is drawn from
the first note to the third and another from the second to the fourth, a cross
is formed. This symbol was established centuries before Bach's time, and he
incorporated it in several subject themes in the WTC. Finally, the melody
closes with a descending chromatic scale—always an intimation of sorrow
and pain.

A further thought to contemplate on the subject theme is that it consists of 11 notes. St. Augustine, who was one of the Church fathers who
laid down certain laws for the interpretation of numbers that remained valid
for centuries, attributed to the number 11 "Transgressionem decalogi notat"
(10 + 1—trespass of the holy Ten Commandments). The subject appears 10
times in the Fugue.

The tonal answer, out of harmonic necessity, cannot, in the first notes,
form the important melodic motif of the subject, and after its statement at
the beginning Bach never again presents this answer theme in the Fugue.

The scene is set, and everything will revolve around the emotional and
spiritual implications of this profound theme.

In developing this Fugue Bach does not employ any contrapuntal
devices of stretti, inversion, augmentation or diminution. Instead, he presents three countersubjects and concentrates on their relationship with the
theme and with each other.

The first countersubject, like the subject, attempts to rise above the
soul's burden, but falls back as though in defeat. The two melodies, at certain points of contact, form the particularly harsh interval—that *Diabolus
in musica*—the tritone, their conjunction stressing the anguish of the theme.
The second countersubject, after a hesitant syncopated start, also rises but
falls back down the scale. The third countersubject is one of those magical
touches so characteristic of Bach. The first three notes form the slow rising
steps of the alto melody heard at the start of the companion Prelude, and
then, it too falls back like all the other themes. It only appears twice in the
Fugue. The first comes in during the fourth statement of the subject at a

symbolically important moment—the beginning of the14th bar. The second
is heard 14 bars later at the 28th. The melody consists of 14 notes. As we
know, the number 14 represents Bach's name in numeral symbolism (B-2,
A-1, C-3, H-8 = 14), and was a kind of personal signature or identification.
He would code this numerical symbol in his music in various ways—14 notes
in a theme, a particularly powerful 14th entry of a subject or something special happening at the 14th bar.

It is most moving when we learn that in his last hours on Earth he dic-
tated to his son-in-law, Altnikol, his final work—the organ Chorale *Vor deinen
Tron tret' ich hiermit* (I come before Thy Throne). Bach used 14 notes for the
first line (symbolizing "I") and for the entire cantus firmus, 41 notes, which
represents J. S. BACH (9 + 18 + 14 =41).

The episodes are of extraordinary beauty. They are like balm for the
soul. There are seven of them—another symbolic implication. From biblical times seven was always known as a holy number.

The mood of all the episodes is expressed through the repetitive anapest
rhythm (♪♪♩). This rhythmic motif defines two different emotional states
in Bach's music. In major keys its character is joyful, lively, and often even
exuberant. One of the best examples is the first movement of the third Brandenburg Concerto.

On the other hand, in minor keys it evokes deep melancholy and calm resignation, pensive and introspective. This rhythm is heard throughout the
Prelude in B-flat minor in Book I. Indeed, there is a close emotional affinity
between that Prelude and this Fugue.

Among the episodes, the sixth is of special spiritual significance. It
begins in bar 43, a number symbolically representing the *Credo* (3 + 17 + 5
+ 4 + 14 = 43), where Bach has modulated to the key of E-flat major—the
Trinity key. Each of the beautiful sequences begins with the rising fourth,
a fundamental religious symbol linked to the symbolism of the Trinity. It is
heard three times.

There is very little ornamentation in the piece, and most important
none on the penultimate note of the subject. This is a reflection of the
solemn tone of the composition. And there is no final climax either. Even

in the double trill and major cadence with which the Fugue closes, one feels there is no release from the soul's burden, but rather a profound sense of resignation.

Prelude, F Minor, Book II

The mood of this lovely Prelude flows directly from the Fugue in the first book, continuing the soul's solitary meditation on the meaning of life's sorrows and burdens. Bach expresses this in music of exquisite simplicity, entirely devoid of technical difficulties. All the musical language is related to a specific affect or emotional dimension.

In the Fugue in this key in the first book we noted that Bach had encoded the symbol for his name, the number 14, in the music. This personal identification appears in this piece, too, this time in the sectional design—an exposition of 28 bars (multiple of 14), a development-like middle section of 28 bars, and a recapitulation of 14 bars.

The Prelude reflects changes appearing on the music scene. It is harmonic and homophonic, looking toward early sonata form. As in so many other Preludes, including the F minor Prelude in Book I, Bach further reveals his ingenious mastery of the broken chord. His perception of its expressive possibilities was virtually unlimited. Here, in particular, the various forms of the chord of the seventh create poignantly beautiful harmonic sequences.

The first section of the opening statement contains a subtle reference to the melodic motif heard at the beginning of the Sinfonia in this key.

In that earlier work, which Bodky described as "one of the most sublime manifestations of Bach's art" (*Interpretation of Bach's Keyboard Works*), agony and despair are expressed to an unprecedented degree. This link with the Sinfonia is significant in forming an interpretation of the Prelude.

The tone of the music is captured immediately with the "sigh motif" in the theme. This falling step motif appears throughout the piece in all the voices. It is heard in many of Bach's choral works, especially in accompaniments to arias depicting deep sorrow and grief. One is the tragic soprano aria *Blute nur, du liebes Herz* (Bleed now, thou dear heart) in the *St. Matthew Passion*, which is about the betrayal of Judas. Note the affinity in the melody of the orchestral part with the thematic motif of the Prelude.

In Bach's time, the chord of the ninth was considered a very disturbing dissonance, and most composers were reluctant to use it. But Bach was never afraid to defy convention. There are times when he used the chord in its solid form to create an acute emotional climax. He also knew that its effect need not always be harsh, but that it had a unique quality which, in broken form, could express deep and intimate feelings of sorrow and longing. It is this quality which we sense in the beautiful sequential passages of bars 20–24 and 62–66, where the interval of the ninth between the soprano and the bass is emphasized on the first beat of each bar in a series of symbolic descending harmonic progressions.

The brooding melancholy rises to the surface in the second section when, after the modulation to B-flat minor, the soprano breaks forth in a soulful melody which reaches almost painful intensity during the wide leaps above a rising chromatic harmonies. There are many examples in Bach's music where rising chromaticism represents painful longing. In the organ Chorale Partita BWV 767 *O Gott, du frommer Gott* (Oh God, thou good God), for the eighth verse of the hymn he wrote a number of variations on the rising chromatic motif in connection with the theme of death and the soul's longing for release and life everlasting.

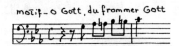

When Bach brings this section to a close, he gives the alto part in the cadence a series of repeated notes. Is this a motivic link to the subject of the companion Fugue where repeated notes will be an important element?

The recapitulation does not intimate that the soul has found any consolation. The anguish remains and, in the final bars, which Keller felt "raises themselves to a painful cry" (*The Well-Tempered Clavier*), reaches a climax on the diminished triads, then subsides on a dark, minor cadence.

Fugue, F Minor, Book II

Few pieces in the collection have elicited more varied and even opposing opinions as to character than this Fugue. Tovey called it a "lively" fugue,
citing the "amusing" characteristics in the episodes and the liveliness the
mordent in the subject adds to "this comedy" (*Bach: 48 Preludes and Fugues,
Book II*, p. 78). Riemann described it as a piece of "bewitching grace and
heart-warming loveliness" (*Analysis of J.S. Bach's Wohltemperirte Clavier*).
Landowska said, "This *perpetuum mobile* has the monotonous intoxication
of a whirling dervish" (*Landowska on Music*, p. 202). J. F. Reichardt, in an
article written in 1782, gave a more detailed and personal account. "The
first time I saw it I could not stop playing it, and it plunged me into the
deepest and yet sweetest melancholy. One might quite well sing words of
deep mourning to it: and it must not be played fast" (David and Mendel,
Bach Reader, p. 456).

In the three other pieces in this key in the WTC the character of the
music is serious and introspective—Bach the inward and very private composer. Perhaps we should keep this in mind when contemplating an approach
to this piece. Whatever the differing interpretations, it is indisputable that
he completed the group with a composition of masterful design and almost
hypnotic beauty.

The subject theme consists of 21 notes, a number signifying three times
holy—the number 7, from biblical times, being a symbol of the Holy Spirit.
It has also been considered a musical translation of the letters S D G (Soli
Deo Gloria), which Bach often wrote at the end of a major work. Of further interest, the subjects of the 1st (C major), the 12th (F minor and midpoint), and the last (B minor) fugues in Book II all have 21 notes.

Another important element in the subject is the subtle association
Bach makes with the companion Prelude. The accented notes—F, E-natu-
ral, B-flat, and A-flat—are all contained within the opening theme of the
Prelude, a thread that carries significant implications. Augmenting this
melancholic "thread" from the Prelude is the falling diminished seventh—
always a symbol of pain and sorrow. During all the entries of the theme,
even in the two places where it is not a diminished seventh (bars 25 and 29)
the second note of that motif always forms a dissonance with its counter-
melody—with one exception. In bar 41, that symbolic number that represents Bach's name, there is a consonance.

As for the opening part of the subject, a melody of a falling fifth followed by a descending diminished seventh, it is perhaps relevant to the
affect of this composition that Bach wrote this melodic pattern for the
flutes at the entry of the choir (bars 19–20) in the first chorus of the *St. John
Passion*.

This Fugue, like the one in this key in the first book, does not display any device of counterpoint, no stretti, inversion, augmentation, etc. But unlike the earlier Fugue which had three countersubjects, for this one Bach gives no countersubject at all. In its stead, he weaves among the theme and through the episodes melodies that continually add to the emotional dimension of the theme while maintaining a unique character of their own.

The most captivating element in this piece is the figure of three repeated notes, and Bach has insisted that it be a central focus of attention. It appears 33 times. The number three, a symbol of the Trinity, is important in Bach's music, and it permeates this Fugue. The subject theme is a multiple of three and that other holy number, 7; there are nine subject entries, and the number of appearances of the three-note figure is again a multiple of this symbolic number. In addition, the three-note motif occurs three times in episodes 2 and 3, at the juncture of episode 4 and the seventh entry of the subject, and in two groups in episode 5, where the second, in bars 22–24, forms with the upper melodies a beautiful and poignant climax. In the coda, which consists of 14 bars—that other signature number representing Bach's name—we again hear it stated three times, this time combined with the powerful resonance of the arpeggiated bass melody.

The Fugue closes with a clear affirmation of inner strength and confidence. Bach has been leading to this right from the beginning.

13

F-Sharp Major

PRELUDE F# major I

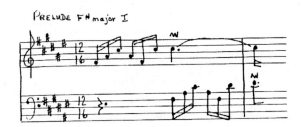

FUGUE F# major I

PRELUDE F# major II

The opportunity to introduce the keys of five, six, and seven flats and sharps to music literature inspired Bach to elicit from these tonalities music of exceptional beauty and emotional impact. The pieces he created in these keys for the WTC are among the greatest in the collection. Those in F-sharp major are very special indeed, for he wrote no other works in this key.

Prelude, F-Sharp Major, Book I

It might seem that Bach took care that the first piece in this relatively difficult key would be fairly easy to play. This may be true to some extent, but as always with Bach, there is much more involved than mere accessibility.

When Bach began the first volume of the WTC he chose for the main motif of the C major Prelude a simple, basic form of the broken chord. And he does so again for the Prelude which begins the second set of 12 keys. In both cases the master's treatment of such an elementary figure evolves in music of such affecting beauty as to defy description.

The compound meter lends a pastoral atmosphere to this Prelude which Geiringer describes as of "serene and peaceful character ... one of the gentlest and most amiable in the set" (*Johann Sebastian Bach: The Culmination of an Era*, p. 281).

Set for only two voices, the simplicity of the design allows for a complete focus on the melody which, with its flute-like quality imbues the whole tone of the piece with a bucolic image. How gently the bass leads this melody through exquisite harmonic progressions to a breathing pause at cadences. And how Bach must have loved, with the new tuning system, gliding to C-sharp major, D-sharp minor, G-sharp minor and A-sharp minor.

What is the essence of the charm of this Prelude? Undefinable, of course, but we can appreciate certain elements which have a definitive role in creating its sublime effect: the rocking motion of the triplet figures, a rhythmic design which Bach would use in the companion Fugue, and in several other pieces in the "introduced" keys; the long melodic sections, glowing with the master's touch; the melodic accent on the off beat, precisely notated for visual recognition by ♪ ♪ instead of tied notes ♩♫♫♩♪

(unless necessary across bar lines), balanced with accents on the beat. Do the alternating upward and downward leaps not evoke a pastoral scene of a flute-playing shepherd and his gamboling flock? And what could perfect this image more than delicate trills and the delightful little joy motif ♫♫ ?

Perhaps this pictorial image can be extended to include a time dimension as well. As the piece approaches the final cadence, the quietude of the low tonality of the melody in bar 25 unfolds with a series of ascending tonic minor and dominant ninth chords from which the melody soars to a glorious climax. A musical depiction, so in keeping with the pastoral theme, of the hush that always precedes sunrise and the elation felt as the sun rises. How else could the piece end but in the spirit of rejoicing? The setting is prepared for the companion Fugue.

Fugue, F-Sharp Major, Book I

Every element in this Fugue—the melodic motifs, rhythmic patterns, contrapuntal interaction—combine to create one of the loveliest musical expressions of pure joy Bach ever conceived. Infused with both vibrant energy and serenity, there is yet another quality at the heart of the piece which captivates us. Is it not, as Stewart MacPherson (*Das Wohltemperirte Klavier*) defined it, "one of the most tenderly beautiful of the whole Forty-eight"?

In the Prelude we noted that Bach began this second set of 12 keys with a figure he used to begin the first set—the broken chord. Now, in this Fugue there is a further affinity, this time of a symbolic nature. The subject, like that of the first Fugue, consists of 14 notes, the numerical symbol for Bach.

The symbolism of numbers fascinated Bach. Scholars have discovered several numbers woven into the design for his compositions, especially the choral works. While many of them are of historic religious origin, his ingenuity extended the range of numbers for symbolic purposes to an extraordinary degree. However he used them, they always had a direct relationship to either the text of a choral work or the "affect" of an instrumental composition. It is no surprise that Bach incorporated the numbers 14 (B A C H) or 41 (J S B A C H) in his symbolic lexicon. It became a secret code that sometimes highlighted particular moments in a piece. But it also was used to intimate a personal identification or association with the spirit of the music. There is no more perfect example, and none more moving, than the Chorale Prelude Bach worked on in his dying hours, *Vor deinen Tron tret' ich hiermit* (I come before Thy throne). To symbolize the *I* Bach used 14 notes for the first line of the hymn and 41 for the entire cantus firmus.

Now let us contemplate the significance of his choosing a theme of 14 notes, and how its character, combined with that of the countermaterial, is enhanced by the hint of a personal "presence."

The pastoral setting prepared in the Prelude now becomes more pictorially vivid. The subject's flute-like melody, adorned with a trill and a joy motif, again places the shepherd at the center of the panorama. The first four notes of the melody become a prominent motif, for Bach singles them out to take part, in canon, in episodes 2, 4, 5, and, most notably, in augmentation at the end of the piece.

In 1716 Bach composed the secular Cantata *Was mir behagt* (BWV 208) known as the Hunting Cantata, which would be a gift from Duke Wilhelm Ernst to Duke Christian von Sachsen-Weissenfels, who was celebrating his 53rd birthday with a hunting party. In the cantata, the opening melody of the seventh aria, *Ein Fürst ist seines Landes Pan* (A prince is the Pan of his country), sung by the bass (Pan), is strikingly relevant to that of the first part of this Fugue's subject. It begins with the same four-note motif, has a rhythmic joy motif, and refers to the mythological flute-playing god of the shepherds.

The countersubject, described by Landowska as of "infinite tenderness" (*Landowska on Music*), is a beautiful flowing melody and surely, among Bach's pictorial themes identified by Schweitzer, one in which "graceful wavy lines depict peaceful rest" (*J.S. Bach*). Bach treats this theme with a fair bit of freedom, slightly altering it several times but never changing its essential character.

The shepherd may well be the central focus, as I mentioned earlier, but he really shares this position with another feature of this idyllic landscape. At bar 7 Bach introduces a "rocking" motif with a pictorial implication so vital to the ambience that from this moment on, there is scarcely a bar in which it does not appear, either in its original form or in inversion. It has been defined as a water motif. Once again we can go to a cantata which, although written much later, affirms this symbolic association.

In 1734 Bach wrote the Cantata BWV 206 *Schleicht, spielende Wellen* (Glide, playing waves), in honor of the birthday of Augustus III. The Elector and his consort were in residence at a merchant's house in Leipzig, where it was performed beneath their windows. Four soloists represent the four rivers (the Vistula, Elbe, Danube, and Pleisse) that flow through the Elector's realm, Saxony and Poland. In the magnificent first chorus three motifs depict various wave motions. The first, heard right at the outset, reveals a definite kinship to the motif in the Fugue.

As a water motif here, its character suggests the image of a little brook bubbling along continuously in the background. Musically, it evokes the spirit of joy and freedom such an image symbolizes.

Returning to number symbolism, we noted earlier that the water motif first appears in the seventh bar. The number 7 has from ancient times held powerful symbolic connotations, of which Bach would certainly have been aware. In alchemical theory 7 is the gateway between Earth and heaven. To the Pythagoreans it was a sacred number and the number of life. And in biblical terms it was the holiest of numbers. Not only does Bach present at bar 7 the motif which will have a dominant effect on the piece, but especially significant is the seventh entry of the theme in the alto. It is a Comes (answer) in the key of B major and thus modified to begin with a perfect fourth as in the Dux (subject), and is the only time it is not accompanied by the countersubject, just the water motif. In addition this occurs at bar 28, a multiple of 14—Bach's numerical symbol for his name.

The piece approaches the end with the soprano singing the last entry of the theme joined by the beautiful countersubject modified in its last notes with a resounding rhythmic joy motif. But the musical image Bach leaves us with in the final cadence is the shepherd and his flute and the song of the brook.

In essence, the Fugue, like the cantatas cited, is also a joyful celebration—of the beauty of nature, of life, and of Creation itself. Which Bach himself invites us to share with him.

Prelude, F-Sharp Major, Book II

Bach begins the second set of 12 keys in the second book with a Prelude consummate in both tonal loveliness and contrapuntal mastery. Like the Prelude in this key in Book I, this too is written for only two voices. Additional voices are added in the closing section for harmonic emphasis and dramatic effect.

The duet form of this Prelude in particular brings into relief the individual character of each of the two main thematic ideas, their combined beauty illuminated by the crystalline quality of the F-sharp tonality.

Bach has made other subtle references to the earlier Prelude—the broken chord which is the basis of the second melodic theme (and its rocking rhythmic effect) and the repeated note figure. Note especially the repeated note with trill in the soprano in bars 26–27—a figure directly from the earlier Prelude. Its ebullient character here is climaxed with a stunning leap spanning a 10th in bar 28—a significant moment for such a spontaneous joyful outburst. And, musically, perfectly designed for Bach to give us a veiled hint of his presence amidst this joy. In Pythagorean theory a perfect number, 28 is also a multiple of 14, the numerical symbol for his name.

The opening theme, accompanied by a dotted rhythm in the French style has an improvisatory feel to it, with graceful ornaments—the slide (Schleifer) and the appoggiatura. There is also a flute-like quality about it, much like the theme of the Fugue in this key in the first book. The melody that follows it evokes a peaceful ambience similar to that of the countersubject in that earlier Fugue. Again, Bach has created a pastoral atmosphere, radiant with joy and contentment. An interesting analogy in both thematic material and pictorial setting of this Prelude and the earlier Fugue can be found in the first chorus of Cantata BWV 7 *Christ, unser Herr, zum Jordan kam* (Christ, our Lord, came to the Jordan), written about 1740.

Although the subject of the chorus has solemn overtones, the melodic theme and wave motif are used for a similar affect, beautifully transmuted for the spirit of the *WTC* pieces.

The Prelude is in six sections to which Bach adds a coda. Each section has its own unique form and variation of the two thematic ideas. The sixth, at bar 57, is marked by the return, with a flourish, of the theme as it was presented at the beginning. Moving through harmonic sequences of extraordinary beauty, the section climaxes at bar 68 with an ornamented cadence on the tonic.

In discussing the F-sharp Fugue in the first book, I suggested that it was a celebration of Creation. Perhaps this hypothesis can be extended to this Prelude. That Bach designed the piece in six sections is worth contemplating. The number six was held by the Pythagoreans to represent the creation of the world, and in biblical reference it had the same symbolic meaning. Bach often put six pieces together under one title—the English Suites, French Suites, Partitas, Brandenburg Concertos, Organ Trios, the Suites for unaccompanied violin and cello. Bodky interpreted this as Bach's homage to the six days of Creation.

With this concept in mind, the evolution of this Prelude, one of Bach's loveliest creations, through six stages to a triumphant conclusion in the coda takes on a deeper dimension with profound implications.

Fugue, F-Sharp Major, Book II

The spirit of this piece, the last in the F-sharp major group in the *WTC*, is full of jubilation. The subject melody sweeps us into this mood immediately with a vibrant trill, moves through a joy motif (♩. ♫ ♩) and concludes with a figure of supreme joy. The alla breve time signature indicates a lively tempo, essential to the mood.

The countersubject, partially formed from the last notes of the subject, dances in perfect partnership with a captivating gavotte rhythm and echoing the trill of the subject.

Particularly intriguing in this Fugue is the melodic figure that forms the focal point of episodes 2 and 4. The motif comes from the end of the subject and from the countersubject. Bach's elaboration of it points to its considerable significance in realizing the affect of the piece. Equally intriguing is that Bach used this motif, also in thirds and sixths, for the Prelude in the immediate preceding key, F minor, seemingly in diametrically opposed emotional contexts. But there is one important difference in its appearance in this piece. Here, the melody has four notes—the drop of a sixth, a key element. I called it a figure of supreme joy. My interpretation derives from Cantata BWV 32 *Liebster Jesu, mein Verlangen* (Dearest Jesus, my longing). In the fifth number, a glorious duet, soprano and bass celebrate the union between soul and Jesus. It is there that we hear the same melodic motif in an expression of supreme joy.

In the concluding section this motif becomes closely integrated, uniting the 9th entry of the subject in the bass to the 10th entry in the alto, marked, as was the 4th entry, by a rhythmic joy motif in the first melodic notes, but paired this time with a trill in the bass. Now comes its finest moments. First, heralding the grand reentry of the soprano, after an absence of several bars, for the exultant final statement of the theme. Then, as a coda, having the definitive role of bringing the Fugue to a jubilant close.

One last thought to leave you with concerns the length of the Fugue— 84 bars. This number is a multiple of 7 and 12, symbolic of "Holy" and

"Creator," respectively. It is also the length of the *Patrem Omnipotentum* in the *B minor Mass*, the great chorus asserting belief in the "Maker of Heaven and Earth and of all things visible and invisible." Bach actually marked the number 84 at the end of this chorus in the autograph.

In the companion Prelude we noted the Creation symbolism associated with the number 6. In fact, the spirit of celebration, of nature and creation, began in the Prelude and Fugue in this key in the first book. If indeed Bach planned the length of this final piece in the group to encompass the ultimate in numerical symbolism related to the Creation theme, it not only reflects his essential character but lifts to empyreal heights the joy and exaltation he expressed through all the pieces in this beautiful tonality in the *WTC*.

14

F-Sharp Minor

115

Bach's keyboard works in this key are rare. The Toccata, the slow movements of the harpsichord and violin sonata in A major, the harpsichord concerto in A major, and the Preludes and Fugues are the only existing pieces. It may be that Bach attributed a uniqueness to this tonality which should not be overexposed but reserved for special moments. Moments of private, intimate emotion. There are several vocal compositions in F-sharp minor in the Cantatas and Bach chose this key for the bass aria "Domine Deus" in the A major *Mass* BWV 234, the *Kyrie eleison* (3) and the *Confiteor* in the B minor *Mass*, and two Passion arias, one in the *St. Matthew* and one in the *St. John*. Close inspection reveals a striking affinity between these Preludes and Fugues and the Passion music. The pervading mood is of sorrowful tenderness and anguish in the contemplation of suffering.

Prelude, F-Sharp Minor, Book I

The opening theme of this Prelude with its descending 16th notes and detached eighth-note pattern has a thematic correspondence with the alto aria *Buss und Reu* (Grief for Sin) in the *St. Matthew Passion*. This aria, which depicts remorse and atonement, also opens with the descending scale and proceeds to a detached eighth-note pattern The falling diminished seventh (always a symbol of pain) in bar 2 of the Prelude occurs in the third entry of the words "Buss und Reu."

In the tenor aria *Ach, mein Sinn* (O, my soul) in the *St. John Passion*, with its cry of anguish and beseeching, a motif of descending 16th notes recurs many times.

The rising leaps in bar 8 and the detached chords in bars 14–15 and bar 19 can certainly be interpreted as cries of remorse, especially the last three that rise as a climax before the music begins its descent and the theme is drawn down to the low bass level. The major chord at the end is comforting.

Fugue, F-Sharp Minor, Book I

In this Fugue are two themes which contain significant elements relating to the Passion music. The subject and countersubject are imbued with the essence of grief and sorrow. The subject, with its faltering steps, conjures up the image of a heavy burden (Jesus carrying the cross?). There are three steps, then three quickened steps and then five more, each set ending with a time suspension. The final six steps clearly stumble onto the long trill and fall to the tonic note. Everything is built into the rhythm pattern— no rubato or other device is needed. A powerful statement contained within a range of only five notes, symbolically intensifying the emotion.

The countersubject consists of the sigh motif—two descending slurred notes, a symbol Bach often used to depict sorrow.

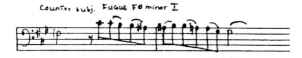

It is found in almost every bar of this Fugue. There can be no mistaking its interpretive implication. Two examples from the *St. Matthew Passion* poignantly illustrate the meaning of this motif. In the Duo e Coro *So ist mein Jesus nun gefangen* (So is now my Jesus taken) where the soprano and contralto sing "Mond und Licht ist vor Schmerzen untergangen" (Moon and light for sorrow hide), the motif is found in both the orchestral and soloists' parts.

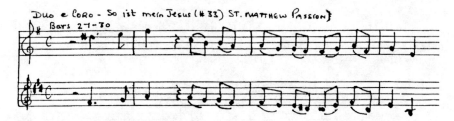

In the chorus that concludes Part I—*O Mensch bewein dein Sünde gross* (O man, thy grievous sin bemoan)—the orchestral music with its constant sigh motif underscores the meaning of the text.

The Fugue movingly expresses the sentiment portrayed in these two excerpts from the Passion.

Prelude, F-Sharp Minor, Book II

This beautiful Prelude is described by Landowska as "a cantilena full of love and tenderness" (*Landowska on Music*). Another scholar finds in it "an outpouring of the inmost soul." The lyric poetry of Bach's musical language transcends time, foreshadowing the melody-focused style of his sons, of Haydn and Mozart, and even further to that of Chopin.

How simply and tenderly the melody begins with the descending interval of the fourth, hauntingly echoed by the middle voice in the next bar. This interval begins the subject of the B-flat minor Fugue in Book I, and we can feel the affinity of mood evoked in both pieces. The tortured pleading in the bass aria *Gebt mir meinen Jesum wieder* (Give me back my Jesus) in the *St. Matthew Passion* begins with a descending fourth.

This melodic motif is the pivot around which the whole Prelude evolves. We are constantly drawn to the inner sorrow by its continual reappearance. It leads us dramatically to the climax at bar 29, culminating on the fermata.

Bach does not often use the fermata within a piece, but when he does it symbolizes an emotional suspension—one can momentarily go no further. The fermata in the B-flat minor Prelude in Book I creates a similar effect (another instance of a connecting thread between the two pieces). There is, however, a definitive example of the symbolic use of the fermata in the aria *Aus Liebe will mein Heiland sterben* (For love will my Saviour die) from the *St. Matthew Passion*. It is found six times, three in the flute solo and three in the soprano part, always over the word *sterben* (die).

There are many other special moments in this Prelude: syncopated passages (often symbolic of weariness in Cantatas); an exceptional harmonic transition in bars 33–34; a rare instance of polyrhythm in bar 15. Suddenly, at the end the rising fourth appears. What could be more comforting than that?

Fugue, F-Sharp Minor, Book II

This magnificent triple Fugue is the consummation of all that has been expressed in the other three pieces. The first subject has three time suspensions, just as the F-sharp minor Fugue in Book I had, but whereas in that Fugue the subject struggles forward and upward, here the melody slowly descends as though in acceptance or resignation and settles more calmly on the long trill and tonic note. In the first five notes the figure of a rising minor sixth falling to the fifth appears. This is a Baroque symbol of pain. When a melody rises an interval of a fifth, moves one step higher to form a minor sixth then falls back one step (P5th–minor 6th–P5th) it is even more symbolic of distress. Bach uses this progression most particularly in the D-sharp minor Fugue in Book I. But notice how this melody proceeds. There, which we heard at the end of the Prelude, is the rising fourth. It is emphasized in the codetta that leads to the third entry of the subject.

The second subject, the utmost in simplicity with its four descending steps, introduces a feeling of strength. In bar 15 there is a hint of this subject. The dotted rhythm is the masterly stroke. Bach allows these two subjects a firm relationship before the third subject enters.

Look closely at the third subject of this Fugue. The motif so resembles the melody of the F-sharp minor Prelude in Book I, one can hardly imagine Bach did not choose this deliberately, but that he wanted to refer back to the beginning and thus unite the four pieces in this key.

At bar 60, all three subjects begin the monumental conclusion—the two Passion-related themes supported by the strong motif. The identical harmony and voicing of the final bars in all four pieces surely connects them, but the striking unison which closes this last piece, with its Renaissance or even medieval sound, becomes the "vanishing point," where all things meet and become one.

15

G Major

PRELUDE G major I

FUGUE G major I

PRELUDE G major II

121

The music in G major pours forth great joy—a joy flowing from a sense of well-being and inner serenity. Bach's greatest source of happiness was, of course, his art, but another vital source was his family. His marriages, by all accounts, were very happy and he took much delight in his children. Anyone who loved music was welcomed to his home and Forkel (his first biographer) tells us that his house was seldom without visitors. He was accessible to others and willing to share his knowledge with sincere listeners, and was certainly interested to learn what was going on in the music world in general.

The Preludes and Fugues in both books and numerous other keyboard pieces express and reflect this joy, happiness and serenity through this key. What a wealth of compositions he chose to write in G major: Invention 10, Sinfonia 10, French Suite no. 5, Partita no. 5, a Toccata, Duetto no. 3, the Goldberg Variations, two organ Preludes and Fugues, and an organ Trio Sonata. Then there is a Sonata for violin and cembalo; a Suite for solo cello; two Brandenburg Concertos... the list goes on.

The choral works abound in magnificent choruses and arias in this key. Some notable ones are Cantata 95, first and last choruses, *Christus, der ist mein Leben* (Since Christ is all my being) and *Weil du vom Tod erstanden bist* (Since thou from death art ris'n again); Cantata 84, soprano aria *Ich esse mit Freuden mein weniges Brot* (I eat my meager bread with joy); Cantata 80, alto/tenor duet *Wie selig sind doch die* (Blessed are they who praise God); Cantata 147, chorus *Wohl mir, dass ich Jesum habe* (It is well for me that I have Jesus)—the famous Jesu Joy melody; Cantata 70, tenor aria *Hebt euer Haupt empor* (Lift high your heads aloft). Hearing any of these great choral works, we grasp the very essence of Bach's music in G major.

Prelude, G Major, Book I

You can dance your way to heaven with this Prelude—that is, if you can survive the trial by fire from bar 13 onward. It is a real pas de deux for the hands, propelled constantly by the broken chord triplets. The implied accent on the off beat is striking, and, as any jazz musician knows, ensures that the music will swing.

Paul Badura-Skoda cites in his book *Interpreting Bach at the Keyboard* (p. 230) a copy of the *WTC* in Leipzig in which Bach added a slur over the a(2)–g(2) in bar 11. Applied and repeated in the other appoggiaturas in the sequence, the rhythm becomes magical.

Perhaps Invention 10 was written around the same time as this Prelude. It certainly goes hand in hand with it, sharing the exuberance.

Fugue, G Major, Book I

You have a pause on the last chord of the Prelude, but that's only to catch your breath. The party's not over. In triple meter, the subject leads off with whirling turns and proceeds to leaps that again accent the off beat. It is joined by a countersubject equally jubilant. A new dance is under way.

As at any festive event, there is so much going on here the mind is dazzled. The fingers get not a moment's rest. The Fugue abounds in contrapuntal devices—inversions, stretti, and episodes that introduce a rocking broken interval pattern which, in contrast to the turns and flashing scales, has a wonderful stabilizing effect.

It is during the development that the excitement noticeably increases. Bach inimitably creates this through rhythmic device. In episode 4, following the modulation to E minor and appearance of both the subject and its inversion, he introduces a 𝅘𝅥𝅯 rhythmic figure. In episode 5, following a modulation to B minor and appearance of the subject in stretto, we hear virtual pirouettes with the turn in ♪♫♫'s by the soprano and bass. This exuberance continues right through to the arrival of the climactic moment in bar 77, when Bach prepares for the grand finale to this joyous occasion. The alto singing a partial inverted theme, and the bass reiterating the inverted turn motif, lead to the exultant final statement of the subject in the soprano, given powerful emphasis by the alto and bass joining in with turns—all heading for the spectacular diminished harmony climax at bar 81. A glorious coda, abundant with ♫ and ♫♫♫ figures, resounding chords rising in harmonic pitch, and an increase in voices, brings the Fugue to a triumphant close. It has been a party to remember.

Prelude, G Major, Book II

As though he were picking up where he left off in the Book I Fugue in this key, Bach starts this Prelude with the rocking broken interval. Here there is a sense of sublimated gaiety. We may not be up dancing, but an inner feeling of well-being and being in tune with the world pervades from start to finish.

From the choral works one interesting example of affinity is worth noting. In the G major bass aria *Gebt mir meinen Jesum wieder* (Give me my Jesus again) in the *St. Matthew Passion*, the same broken interval pattern is found in the accompaniment. The correspondence lies in key tonality and rhythmic energy rather than sentiment.

Of particular importance is the descending tonic scale in the last bar of this Prelude. The figure is prominent in many other works in G major. Its rock-solid key affirmation and strong sense of purpose is echoed in the first bar of the Toccata.

The scale begins the Courante in the fifth French Suite, lighter in effect and rhythmically perfect for the dance form. Another dance, the Allemande from the fifth Partita starts with the same motif, graceful in its rhythmic variation.

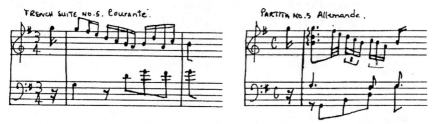

Last but not least, Bach chose this specific melody to open the fifth Partita.

Fugue, G Major, Book II

We are truly in the midst of a great celebration and the dancing is in full swing. The subject, a long one of five and a half bars, consists entirely of broken chords. Much more vigorous and lively than the broken chord pattern of the Prelude.

If the subject's theme reminds you of another piece of Bach's, you're right. The opening melody of the Corrente in the fifth Partita is almost identical.

The number 6 is symbolically important in Bach's music. Many of his works form groups of six: the Brandenburg Concertos, the Sonatas and Partitas for solo violin, the Suites for solo cello, the Sonatas for violin and clavier, the organ Trio Sonatas, the clavier Partitas, French Suites, and

English Suites. There are six entries of the subject in this Fugue. This number is Bach's reference to the six days of creation. Within the concept of such a wondrous cosmic event lies the element of jubilation, which is the essence of this Fugue.

Another revealing motif is the interval of the fourth, a fundamental religious symbol, which occurs in bars 10 and 12. Taking part in the festivity, the leaps of the fourth are rhythmically accented by a mordent on the off beat. They are an important link with the Prelude which has a similar figure in bars 33–34 . Joyous jumps of the sixth.

In the G major Prelude Book I, I mentioned the aria *Gebt mir meinen Jesum wieder*, wherein the broken interval melodic pattern occurs in both pieces. A further correspondence lies between the beautiful violin solo in that aria and this Fugue—broken chords and ♩♩♩♩ note melodies.

Thus we have three motifs apparently indigenous to the key tonality, serving a unified purpose in the Preludes and Fugues but a quite different pictorial role in the aria, which portrays Judas's remorse over his betrayal. It is one of many examples of Bach's genius in transforming specific elements within a common tonality so that the character remains yet the musical effect is subtly altered.

But Bach's intent is clearly defined throughout the G major set in the WTC—to impart supreme joy.

A brilliant coda, incorporating the final subject entry and ending with the signature descending G major scale, concludes this momentous occasion.

16

G Minor

PRELUDE   G minor I

FUGUE G minor I

PRELUDE G·minor II
LARGO

Bach knew only too well about personal grief and sorrow. At just 10 years old he had already lost both parents. After 13 years of marriage, his first wife died suddenly while he was in Carlsbad with Prince Leopold. One can scarcely imagine the devastating effect he experienced on his return, entering his home completely unaware of what had happened. Of his 20 children, 11 died during his lifetime, 1 son at age 24 in 1739 and the others either in infancy or early childhood. One son, who was mentally deficient, survived his father by several years, but undoubtedly needed much care and attention during the 26 years before Bach's death.

We have no record of Bach communicating his feelings about the tragedies in his life. One letter of October 28, 1730, to Georg Erdmann (David and Mendel, *Bach Reader*, p. 125) simply states that his first wife died in Cöthen. For Bach, music was the supreme language whereby the experiences of life could be expressed. His sorrow was lifted to the universal realm.

That Bach often chose the key of G minor to convey this human experience is borne out by many arias, choruses and recitatives in the Cantatas and the Passions. The Preludes and Fugues in this key all contain elements that relate directly to sorrow, grief, pain and despair as depicted in the choral works

Prelude, G Minor, Book 1

The first chorus (in G minor) of the *St. John Passion* haunts the opening of this Prelude with the repeated tonic note in the bass. The mood evoked is similar in both pieces and draws us gently into the contemplative character of the music.

The music that unfolds in the Prelude is a study in ornamentation, in particular, the slide and the turn. But of course, Bach goes far beyond these simple ornaments to create a melody which, combined with angularity of interval and syncopation, is as expressive of sorrow as the soprano aria *Zerfliesse, mein Hertz in Fluten der Zähren* (Release, my heart, thy torrents of crying) from the *St. John Passion*, with its slides and turns accompanied by repeated bass notes.

Syncopation in step motifs often expressed weariness, the desire for release from burdens. Its appearance early in the piece is symbolically significant. In fact, the whole sentiment of the Prelude is established in the first few bars.

Fugue, G Minor, Book I

Both the subject and countersubject in this Fugue continue to reflect the pain and grief inherent in the Prelude. The subject contains 11 notes, a number that carries its own symbolic reference. St. Augustine attributed to the number 11 *Transgressionem decalogi notat* (10 + 1 = trespass of the Holy Commandments). In F minor, the other key that Bach chose to express deep suffering, the subject of the Fugue in Book I has 11 notes. Comparing these two subject themes provides us with a deeper insight into the music of both pieces.

The melody of the first half of the subject appears in at least two Cantatas and is set to words that give this motif a significant character. In Cantata 106 *Gottes Zeit ist die allerbeste Zeit*, the chorus *Es ist der alte Bund* (It is the old oath—Man, thou art to die!) is based on this motif (in slightly altered form). This Cantata dates from 1707 or 1711, so was written before the Fugue. We find the theme again in Cantata 89 *Was soll ich aus dir machen, Ephraim?*, in the aria *Ein unbarmherziges Gerichte* (A merciless judgment) which dates from 1730—after the Fugue. It appears that Bach purposely recalled this melody.

The second part of the subject is characterized by its rhythm ♩ ♫ ♫ ♪ which also becomes the motif for the countersubject. It is relentless in its insistence, occurring in every bar except 11 and 33. In the chorus *Bist du nicht* from the *St. John Passion*, the orchestra creates almost unbearable tension with this incessant rhythm during the taunting of Peter.

Although there seems to be no relief here either, Bach has an extraordinary design. The Fugue is in four voices, yet in only two passages do they all sound together. These are moments of considerable emotional impact. The first instance forms the midpoint climax at bars 15–18. But during the coda Bach not only includes all four voices but adds a fifth voice as well, creating a sensation of surging inner strength, culminating on the major tonic chord.

Prelude, G Minor, Book II

If Bach used defining symbols for grief and anguish in the first Prelude and Fugue, the rhythmic motif used throughout this Prelude is even more ominous in its implications. It is found in so many instances in the Passions that its interpretation cannot be mistaken. It always expresses extreme distress and even terror, horror and despair. The very short notes will have a piercing character and will carry the emotional intensity from beginning to end.

It is worth noting here that Handel, in the *Messiah*, also used this rhythm for a similar purpose in the solo *He gave His back to the smiters* and in the chorus *Surely, He hath borne our griefs*.

In the alto recitative *Erbarm es Gott!* (Have pity, God!) from the *St Matthew Passion*, the accompaniment consists entirely of this motif. She sings *O Geisselung* (Oh scourging); *O Schläg* (Oh smiting); *O Wunden* (Oh wounds) in this declamation that leads to the great G minor aria *Können Tränen meiner Wangen* (If my tears be unavailing) where the motif continues.

Another aria in which this rhythm underlines the text is the bass solo
Komm, süsses Kreuz (Come, sweet cross).

As the Passion nears its conclusion, Bach chooses G minor for the bass
recitative *Am Abend da es kühle war* (At evening when it was cool), which still
is imbued with sorrow but "peace in understanding" surrounds the music.
It is also the key of the recitative that tells of the burial.

The final phrase of this Prelude is poignant with a sudden plaintive
cry in the soprano as the melody leaps up a minor seventh and remains in
the high register to the end.

Fugue, G Minor, Book II

This magnificent Fugue develops from a subject that consists of two
musical ideas that carry special significance. The first four notes form the

cross motif, a symbol used long before the Baroque era. If lines are drawn from the first to the fourth note and from the second to the third, a cross appears. Bach forms this pattern in other fugal subjects in the collection. Another prominent element in the melody is the interval of the fourth, a historically established fundamental religious symbol. The last section of the subject is a melodic theme that Bach used much earlier (1714) in the opening chorus of Cantata 21 *Ich hatte viel Bekümmernis* (I had many sorrows).

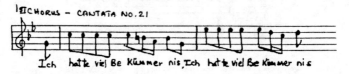

Bach returned to this melody again, using it note for note in an organ fugue, but transforming its musical affect by a major tonality. A wonderful example of his ingenuity and perceptivity.

An interesting example of a similar repeated note pattern is in the chorus *Lasset uns den nicht zerteilen* (Let us then not cut or tear it) from the *St. John Passion*. It emphasizes the agitated dialogue among the soldiers about Jesus' coat.

Elements from all three of the previous pieces in this key are woven into the plan of this Fugue: the repeated note pattern from the Book I Prelude; a rhythmic motif as insistent in its repetition as the one in the Book I Fugue; a dotted figure distilled from the Book II Pre-

lude. As Bach combines them with the thematic material of this composition in an awesome display of contrapuntal mastery, the music reaches a
magnitude of epic dimensions. Suffering, grief and despair undergo a metamorphosis.

That this Fugue is 84 bars in length is particularly symbolic. It was discovered that at the end of the chorus *Patrem omnipotentum* in the *B minor
Mass*, Bach had written the number 84. It is the multiple 7 times 12, 7 being
the symbol for holy, grace of God, and 12 representing the Apostles, devotees.

The Fugue in G minor Book II is surely a testament to faith and courage—steadfastness amidst adversity.

17

A-Flat Major

PRELUDE Ab major BK.I

FUGUE Ab major BK.I

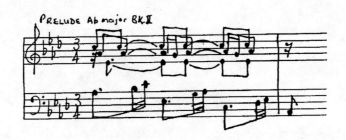

PRELUDE Ab major BK.II

To the key of A-flat major Bach bestowed majesty, dignity, grandeur, serene confidence, and joy. Each of the Preludes and Fugues in the *WTC* is characterized by one or more of these qualities. It is a key seldom found in Bach's compositions, and we can expect the rare instances to be of significant import.

Such is the case in two numbers from the *St. Matthew Passion*. One, of cosmic dimensions, is the chorus (no. 63) *Wahrlich, dieser ist Gottes Sohn gewesen* (Truly, this was the Son of God), which follows the recitative describing the cataclysmic events after the crucifixion.

The other is the sublime, serene Recitativo e Coro *Nun ist der Herr zur Ruh gebracht* (Now is the Lord brought to rest), which begins in A-flat major and modulates through to C minor for the final chorus. A truly noble key.

Prelude, A-Flat Major, Book I

Opening with strong key-affirming chords like an orchestral overture, the theme, with its rhythmic joy motif ♪♫ ♫ basically consists of six notes. The symbolic meaning, to Bach, of the number six has been interpreted as his homage to the six days of creation. Or in abstract terms, a celebration of life itself.

There are several examples where Bach put together pieces of the same genre in groups of six: six English Suites, six French Suites, six Partitas, six Brandenburg Concertos, six organ Trios, six Sonatas and Partitas for solo violin, and six Suites for solo cello. Within the 44 bars of this Prelude, the rhythmic joy motif occurs 36 times, itself a multiple of 6.

The marvel of Bach's skill in this piece is that the constant repetition of the thematic motif never becomes monotonous. The secret lies in the wonderful series of melodic patterns in counterpoint to the motif. All of them, in their uniqueness, magnify the exuberance which Bach intended us to share with him.

In the final section Bach brings the joy motif into focus as directly as in the beginning, illuminating the deep sense of well-being even further with the rich sound of a passage of *batteries*, and the addition of ornaments to the theme. The seal of the master.

Fugue, A-Flat Major, Book I

Bach began the Prelude with the key-affirming A-flat triad and does so here to open the companion Fugue. There is a serene dignity in the simplicity of the subject melody, and the whole Fugue is one of quiet meditation. Numerical symbolism is again found in Bach's chosen theme. It consists of seven notes. The number 7 historically represented the word *holy* and extended further to include the wonder of creation. Reference to this number is found throughout Bach's music and in many cases even multiples of it. Two important examples of the latter are found in the *B minor Mass*: the *Et incarnatus est* is 49 bars (7 times 7) in length, and the *Patrem Omnipotentum*, which is 84 bars (7 times 12, 12 also being a holy number—the Apostles, devotees) in length. In fact Bach actually wrote the number 84 at the end of this chorus in the autograph. The celebratory spirit of the Prelude has now become contemplative in the Fugue.

It is interesting that there is no definitive countersubject here. The melody that Bach introduces with the second entry only appears again in exact imitation in the short episode between the second and third entries of the subject. Motifs from this melody appear throughout the Fugue, but it never exactly returns as he presented it at the beginning. If we think back to the Prelude, we remember that that theme was paired with several melodic patterns. Perhaps Bach had the same design in mind for the Fugue. What is clear is that these beautiful melodies, flowing continuously throughout, affect the character of the theme and the overall ambience of the music in an extraordinary way. The episodes in particular are exceptionally moving.

The penultimate entry of the subject at bar 30 with its sequential repetition of the last three notes leads us to the sublime climax from which the final entry, regal with its chords, and which Bach has ornamented with a mordent and, most important, now forms the rhythmic joy motif of the Prelude, brings the Fugue to a close. A serene cadence, magically affected by the alto melody.

Prelude, A-Flat Major, Book II

As in the pieces in A-flat major in Book I, Bach opens this Prelude with the key-affirming tonic chord. But what an imposing statement this is—full of majesty and stateliness. The tone of this chordal motif is ennobled by the accompanying figure in the bass. This is not just a broken chord but is recognized as the *Sanctus* (Holy) symbol, the falling octave which permeates the great *Sanctus* of the *B minor Mass*. The octave can also be filled with notes of the major chord, which Bach did when Jesus "speaks" in the recitative *Du sagst's ich bin ein König* (Thou sayest I am a King) in the *St. John Passion* and in the recitative *Setzet euch hie* (Sit ye here) in the *St. Matthew Passion*.

Not only has Bach chosen a distinctive form of this symbol for this Prelude, but it appears seven times, the historical numerical symbol for holy. Of added significance, the piece itself is 77 bars in length.

We noted that the subject of the A-flat Fugue in Book I contained seven notes. There is further affinity between the sets in the two books. Both Preludes are written in two-part and are orchestral in style. This prelude is particularly reminiscent of the French-style Ouverture with its dotted rhythm. It is designed with a series of tutti with extended passages for the two soloists.

A quiet dignity pervades throughout this long Prelude. It is Bach's sheer virtuosity of inventiveness, the subtle placements of the moving part in the chordal motifs, the elegant elaboration of the soloists' melodies and the seemingly effortless beautiful harmonic modulations which sustain the emotional intensity through the gentle pace of the music.

Stravinsky, in a conversation with Robert Craft, remarked that in listening to Handel's *Balshazzar* he never experienced the "....wonderful jolts, the sudden modulations, the unexpected harmonic changes, the deceptive cadences, that are the joy of every Bach cantata" (Stravinsky and Craft, *Expositions and Developments*, p. 64). All of these abound in the *WTC*, too. In the final section of the Prelude we hear exactly what Stravinsky was talking about. Who would imagine that Bach would lead us to the climactic moment we've been waiting for with a modulation to B-double-flat major! A dramatic run up that scale pivots on a Neapolitan sixth. And there we are—on the dominant seventh of A-flat major. What a homecoming! Direct, firm, and just one beat and no fermata on the last chord!

Fugue, A-Flat Major, Book II

Bach has matched the majestic Prelude with a Fugue of equal grandeur. The pervading mood throughout is one of serene exaltation, the musical language rich in symbolism.

The subject consists of 20 notes, a multiple of the number 5. This number is historically assigned to the crucifixion, connoting the five wounds inflicted on Jesus. Within the Fugue there are 15 appearances of the subject. In this context the opening motif is highly significant. The first four notes of the subject form the cross symbol, which appears when a line is drawn from the first to the fourth notes and from the second to the third notes. In addition, Bach has included in the theme the drop of the octave—the *Sanctus* (holy) symbol, which was so definitive in the Prelude.

The first countersubject is entirely in keeping with the contemplative character of the subject. The descending chromatic scale always denotes sorrow and pain but notice that Bach completes this theme with the positive rising fourth—in itself a historical religious symbol. A lifting of the spirit uniting with the reassuring flowing melody of the last section of the subject.

The second countersubject , introduced at the third entry, is never strictly adhered to but flows in free form throughout. Beginning at bar 10 a variation motif of this melody is given an unusually long sequential passage. Yet when we examine it closely, it appears that Bach fully intended the motif to appear seven times—another holy symbol integral to the pieces in A-flat major.

Although this is a four-voice Fugue, it is particularly interesting that the predominant number of voices heard together is three. Even in the exposition at the fourth entry of the subject the soprano is dropped. The number 3 is another holy symbol, representing the Trinity, and Bach makes symbolic reference to it many times in his works. In this Fugue, besides the dominance of three-voice counterpoint, he has, at bars 26–27, written the *Sanctus* drop of the octave three times in the soprano, often emphasized by performers. But what is especially significant is that Bach has brought the four voices together only three times—at bars 22, 37 and 42. This last instance is truly extraordinary. It is the 14th entry of the subject and we know that at a 14th entry in a Fugue something special happens. For this number represents Bach's name—B-flat-2, A-1, C-3, H(B natural)-8 = 14. With the subject now accompanied by an ornamented first countersubject he begins the spectacular modulation to B-double-flat major which was so electrifying in the companion Prelude. A resounding cadenza, like those found in the great organ works, leads through the Neapolitan sixth to the climax on the A-flat dominant seventh.

Now, the coda. *Three* elements contribute to the power and beauty of the finale. In the middle of bar 48 we hear an echo of the rhythm of the chordal motif of the Prelude.

The 15th entry of the subject in the same bar is given to a *fifth* voice, and an affecting alto melody (which was also Bach's design for the end of the A-flat major Fugue in Book I) leads all the voices to the great six-voice final chord.

Bach often stressed to his pupils that a composition should not be judged predominantly by the impression of its performance but by the merits of the musical score. In these pieces in A-flat major, the score reveals so much more than can be heard in performance. Indeed, marvelous things to contemplate, be aware of, and to listen for, far beyond the notes on the page.

Numerology, dating from antiquity, fascinated Bach all his life, and he firmly believed in it. The marvel is his ingenious translation of that esoteric science into the language of music. Bodky summed it up when he wrote, "That he could build the mathematical calculation of number symbolism into his design without hindering the spontaneity and depth of expression is beyond understanding" (*Interpretation*, p. 255).

18

G-Sharp Minor

PRELUDE G# minor I

FUGUE G# minor I

PRELUDE G# minor II

It is the keys with five, six and seven sharps or flats which he intro-duced to the keyboard repertoire that inspired Bach to an extraordinary de-gree. All the Preludes and Fugues in these keys in the *WTC*, especially those in Book II, are among the greatest in the collection, consummate in har-monic and melodic beauty, depth of expression, and mastery of the art form.

Bach captures the unique quality of the G-sharp minor tonality and molds it ingeniously to the specific affection he intends for each piece. These works hold a special place in his music—he wrote no other compositions in this key.

Prelude, G-Sharp Minor, Book I

Within the graceful charm and tenderness of this Prelude lie intima-tions of a darker nature. The theme itself seems tinged with an aura of melancholy. The motif formed in the first six notes is the soul of the Pre-lude. It appears in every bar either in imitation, inversion, or permutation. It is magical how Bach elicits from this simple melody its full potential for emotional expression.

There are four elements which play a vital role in the emotional dynam-ics of the piece. The movement through a diminished triad from the first motif to the last part of the theme. This progression is maintained in the inversion of the theme, creating another dimension. The sigh motif (two descending slurred notes, first appearing in bar 7 and annotated by Bach himself) is also important. The falling interval of a diminished seventh, an historical symbol of sorrow and pain is one of the elements. Finally, there is the repeated-note figure, which will form a link with the companion Fugue. It is the last two which create the powerful climax at bars 24–25.

Bach often made a subtle personal identification in his music through the symbolic number 14. This represents his name when the alphabetical positions are added together—B-flat-2, A-1, C-3, H(B-natural-8). He did this in various ways such as 14 notes in a theme, a particularly striking 14th entry of a fugal theme, or something special occurring at the 14th bar. In this piece the 14th bar draws our attention. It is approached by the only trill in the composition, it contains the first appearance of the main motif in duet, and it is the place where the music has modulated to the most extreme key of D-sharp minor. This marks the midpoint from which the tension will gradually build to the climax. We are made even more aware of Bach's presence as the music draws to a close. The penultimate bar is the 28th, a multiple of 14, in which the alto sings the inverted theme but the melody has been altered to form a descending diminished seventh chord—an even stronger symbol of distress than the diminished seventh interval. Bach also adds here a second alto voice which is often phrased in sigh motifs.

A beautiful Prelude. It is Bach communicating with us on a very intimate and personal level.

Fugue, G-Sharp Minor, Book I

From November 6 to December 2, 1717, Bach was confined to jail in Weimar by Duke Wilhelm Ernst as a result of a heated confrontation over his request for dismissal so that he could take up a new position at the court in Cöthen. Bach's punishment was all the more unreasonable in that the real motive behind the whole affair lay in a family feud between the two courts. Duke Wilhelm simply did not want to lose Bach to his detested relatives in Cöthen. The humiliation and feeling of injustice that Bach suffered can hardly be underestimated.

Guided by a comment written in 1791 by E. L. Gerber, the son of H. N. Gerber, who was one of Bach's pupils, some scholars believe that it was during this enforced solitude that Bach did considerable work on the first book of the *Well-Tempered Clavier*. If we approach this Fugue from the standpoint that it may have been conceived under these circumstances, many elements in the music which define its character become very relevant. First of all, there is the key itself. Perhaps Bach chose this difficult key to portray a difficult situation. The thematic material and rhythmic motifs strengthen this hypothesis.

In the Prelude we detected a symbolic reference to his name in the number 14. He also identified himself in his music through the number 41. This number is arrived at with the addition of J S to the letters B A C H— J-9 (J and I were the same letters in his time) and S-18 + 14 = 41. With its length of 41 bars, this Fugue is surely a testament of a personal nature but, as always with Bach, speaks to universal experience.

Both the beginning and the end of the Prelude form a direct melodic link with its companion Fugue. The first five notes of the bass melody in the Prelude become the first five notes of the Fugue's subject, and in the final bars of the Prelude the last four notes of the inverted theme in the alto form this motif, which is immediately heard in the opening tenor statement of the subject, thus establishing the relationship between the two pieces.

This motif, however, is now rhythmically changed to create a very different mood. Beginning with a strong thrust on a normally weak beat. the long first note presages the combative tone of the whole Fugue.

The first seven notes of the subject closely resemble the melody of the first line of the Chorale *Verleih' uns Frieden gnädiglich* (Grant us peace by thy mercy) which closes Cantata 126.

Not only are these words of the chorale a fitting supplication but the last five lines seem particularly relevant: *Gib unsern Fürst'n und aller Obrigkeit / Fried' und gut Regiment / Dass wir unter ihnen / ein geruh'g und stilles Leben führen mögen / In aller Gottseligkeit und Ehrbarkeit* (Give our princes and all in authority / peace and order / that we under them / may lead a quiet and peaceful life / with righteousness and honesty).

The strong, assertive character of the subject is further developed by a leap of a tritone, that "diabolus in musica," and firmly established in the final section by a heavy repeated-note figure.

The disturbing, even threatening effect which can be created by the tritone is clearly illustrated by Bach in two numbers from the *St. Matthew Passion*: the alto's final two notes in the grief-stricken recitative no. 59 *Ach, Golgatha*, and in the taunting words of the crowd in chorus no. 61 *Halt, lass sehen, ob Elias komme, und ihm helfe* (Let be, let us see whether Elias will come to save him).

Near the end of the Prelude, an emotionally charged series of repeated-note chords form the climax. A repeated-note step motif now becomes the driving force dominating the whole Fugue. It appears 24 times.

The aggressive character of the subject is augmented by a countersubject consisting of two strong rhythmic motifs— 𝅘𝅥𝅮𝅘𝅥𝅮𝅘𝅥 𝅘𝅥𝅮𝅘𝅥𝅮𝅘𝅥 and 𝅘𝅥𝅮𝄾𝅘𝅥𝅮𝄾𝅘𝅥𝅮, the latter strategically placed during the exposition to sound in conjunction with the repeated-note figure. Indeed, in the fourth entry of the subject, in the bass, Bach adds fuel to the fire by leading the other voices to full chords on the 𝅘𝅥𝅮𝄾𝅘𝅥𝅮𝄾𝅘𝅥𝅮 motif, and, rising in pitch, sequentially repeats the passage two more times. Another instance where this type of motif, appearing as 𝅘𝅥𝄾𝅘𝅥𝄾𝅘𝅥 plays an important role is in the B-flat minor Fugue in Book II, a fugue of great magnitude portraying inner conviction.

The modulation to D-sharp minor at the end of the exposition marks a release of tension—the bass voice is dropped and the sequential repetition gently descends in the approach to C-sharp minor.

A second countersubject appears at the third entry of the subject and is of a more peaceable nature.

The melody is formed from the first section of the subject but has been given a gentle syncopated rhythm. Could we say it is the intermediary between the two antagonists? Take note of when it appears. Bach brings it in only five times, but in the third and fifth it is prominently in top position.

In the approach to the end of the Fugue, Bach returns to the aggressive repeated-note step motif, stating it authoritatively in a climactic rising sequential pattern, the last of which, in the bass, is accented by a defiant drop of a diminished seventh—the dramatic interval which brought the Prelude to its climax.

The Fugue ends on a minor chord (although some artists play a major). If this minor cadence is indeed what Bach intended, being the only instance in Book I, it is symbolically significant in relation to the affection of the piece.

Bach never tolerated injustice. This superb Fugue reflects determination and courage, qualities which in his own life never failed him. He did go to Cöthen and his years there proved to be among the happiest of his life.

Prelude, G-Sharp Minor, Book II

Although many years separate the completion of each volume of the WTC, with close study it becomes evident that Bach referred to what he had written in a certain key in the first book while designing and composing the pieces in the same key in the second. In subtle and ingenious ways he demonstrated his intention to connect the Preludes and Fugues in both books, creating a kind of experiential emotional journey.

Several motivic patterns that are important to the character of the earlier set have been brought forward to this Prelude and skillfully woven within the new material.

The aura of melancholy which is felt in the earlier Prelude still hovers in the atmosphere of this one, but it is by no means a gloomy mood nor is there any trace of the aggression and combativeness of the earlier Fugue.

Consisting of two sections, foreshadowing early sonata form, the tone of the Prelude is immediately set forth in the opening statement—a beautiful undulating melody followed by the unmistakable symbol of pathos in Bach's music—the sigh motif. Bach adds to the emotional dimension of this opening statement by repeating it with the sigh motifs in a higher pitch and intervals of the sixth—and specifically marked *piano*. Adding to the effect of the sigh motif is the "rocking" figure which accompanies it. Bach seems to have had a predilection for a rocking figure in his Preludes in keys with five or more sharps or flats in Book II. We find it in the C-sharp major, the E-flat minor, the F-sharp major, and the B major. In all cases the figure has a profound influence on the affection of the composition.

The sigh motif was specifically indicated by Bach in the Book I Prelude, and here he has given it an equally prominent role. Not only is it part of the main theme but it is formed in the bass melodic figure which first appears beginning at bar 8, then again early in the second section, also in the bass, and last in the soprano just before the recapitulation. The symbolic connotation of the sigh motif is heightened in the sequential repetition of this melodic figure by a descending chromatic progression. This melodic figure comes directly from the Fugue in the first book during the seventh subject entry at bar 18.

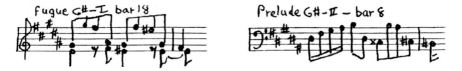

The aggressive rhythmic motif ♪ ⅞ ♪ ⅞ ♪, which is an important element in the Fugue in the first book, appears early in this Prelude, right at the point where Bach has indicated a *forte,* but note how Bach has transformed its character by syncopation and two little 16ths ⅞♪ ⅞♪ ⅞♫. In the Fugue, at the end of the exposition, the figure was sequentially repeated twice to augment its affect—and now Bach does the exact same thing with the motif in its new form, sequentially repeating it twice for the same purpose. Perhaps if we stop for a moment and reflect that the earlier Fugue was written when Bach was in his thirties and this Prelude probably when he was in his mid- to late fifties, this change from the aggressive character of the motif to a more gentle one deepens our perceptions and intuitive response to the music.

Later in the first section it appears once (bar 19) in the ♪⅞♪⅞♪ form but returns to the syncopated form before the cadence. In the second section Bach reserves it for the Prelude's closing moments.

In the second section are two other important motifs—one not heard in the earlier set and the other a crucial element in both its Prelude and Fugue. The first is a rhythmic motif in the bass occurring only in bars 29 and 30, ⅞♫♫ ♫, which Schweitzer (*J. S. Bach*) identified as a "rhythm of felicity." It is a motif which, in various forms, often appears in choral works where the theme is trusting acceptance and faith. It is significant that this passage modulates to the Trinity key of A major.

Between this motif and the second one there is something else you must not miss. In the earlier Prelude and Fugue Bach wrote a falling diminished seventh interval (a symbol of pain and sorrow) at decisive moments in each piece. We also found there a personal reference through the symbolic numbers 14 and 41. Right at the start of the recapitulation of this Prelude Bach has written, in counterpoint to the main theme, a bass melody that ends with a pronounced drop of the diminished seventh. Not only is this at a vital moment in the composition, but it is at bar 41—the symbolic number representing his name, J. S. Bach!

The second important motif in the second section is the repeated-note figure. As I mentioned above, this figure has a dynamic role in both the earlier Prelude and Fugue. But it is its role in that Prelude which Bach carries forward to this Prelude. In both pieces, six bars before the end, it brings the music to a poignant climax. What is particularly affecting here is that after the climax the motif continues to reverberate through the tension-releasing descending harmonic progression, and on reaching its lowest depth goes through a metamorphosis—a descending chromaticism leading to what seems inevitable—a minor cadence.

A Prelude exquisite in charm and beauty.

Fugue, G-Sharp Minor, Book II

Bach's journey through the tonality of G-sharp minor now culminates in a magnificent double Fugue. It is a long work divided into three distinct sections: the development of the first theme, the development of the second theme, and then the combination of the two themes.

The quintessential nature of the composition lies in the contrasting character of these two themes—one purely diatonic and the other entirely chromatic. Each has its own emotional dimension, yet their juxtaposition creates a sublime ambience.

In retrospect we see that the mood of the first three pieces in this key alternated between different aspects of melancholy and combativeness. In this last piece of the group one senses an atmosphere bordering on nostalgia—a looking back in quiet reflection. From a chronological viewpoint this could be interpreted as a natural evolution of mood when we consider that Bach composed this in the later years of his life.

It is highly significant that Bach develops each of the themes at length before the ultimate blending of the two emotional experiences. Nostalgia is by nature a combination of bittersweet memories. The benign and gentle melody of the first theme sets the tone of the music. Its lilting compound meter induces a reminiscent mood of happiness and contentment. Bach allows us to savor and absorb the affect of this melody by developing it at length (61 bars) and enhancing it with beautiful contrapuntal melodies and episodic interludes. Yet we cannot fail to notice that he has introduced the darker element implied by chromaticism at the second entry of the subject. It does not take part in the third entry. This foreshadows the second subject and undoubtedly signals the important role chromatic thematic material will play. It will prove to lie deep at the heart of the Fugue. Apropos of this chromatic countersubject, there is a little moment about halfway through this section that is strikingly poignant. During the episode following the fourth entry of the subject, in bar 26 there is a diminished third in the melody—an interval often associated with pain in Bach's choral works. He used it sparingly and only when it would be most meaningful.

Now, when Bach begins the development of the second theme alone in the second section he introduces in counterpoint to it a "brighter" element, a little rhythmic joy motif ♫ ♩, along with more extended 16th figures.

Let's look more deeply into the implications of descending and ascending chromatic melodies. The former has always been a symbol of sorrow and grief. Two examples from Bach's choral works illustrate his use of this melodic figure to depict these sentiments in a specific context. In Cantata 4 *Christ lag in Todesbanden* (Christ lay in the bonds of death), a descending chromatic scale begins the accompaniment to the bass chorale *Hier ist das rechte Osterlamm* (Here is the real Easter Lamb). The message of the text is redemption through suffering. The second is the bass figure, repeated 13 times, of the *Crucifixus* of the *B minor Mass*.

The ascending chromatic figure in many of his works expresses hope and longing for release from suffering. In Cantata 131 *Aus der Tiefe rufe ich, Herr, zu dir* (Out of the depths I cry, Lord, to Thee), the figure appears in the fifth chorus accompanying the words *Und er wird Israel erlösen aus allen seinen Sünden* (And He will redeem Israel out of all its sins).

In the same context of hope and longing, Bach wrote a series of variations on this motif in an organ Chorale Partita BWV 767 based on the eighth verse of the hymn *O Gott, du frommer Gott* (O God, Thou good God)— expressing the longing for resurrection after death.

A last quote from Bach's works is particularly revealing and relevant. In the final bars of the Adagissimo (sometimes referred to as a lamento) in the *Capriccio on the Departure of a Most Beloved Brother* BWV 992, both the descending and ascending chromatic figures appear in the same sequence as in the theme of the second subject of this Fugue.

There is one section of special significance where Bach prominently emphasizes the ascending chromatic motif. In the episode beginning at bar 83 a series of sequential imitations of it proceeds from voice to voice with the bass repeating it four extra times—a total of seven—a symbolic holy number. This seventh statement of the motif is given special treatment. It is separated from the others by two bars and is accompanied by the little joy motif rhythm in the alto. The import of this passage takes on an added dimension when we realize Bach designed this as the approach to the ultimate moment in the Fugue—the union of the two main themes.

In the first three pieces in this key we detected motivic patterns carried forward as subtle but important links between them. In this last piece, Bach makes only fleeting reference to what came before. The first three notes which begin the first subject are the same notes that form the beginning of both the Preludes in Book I and Book II. Then that important rhythmic motif heard throughout the Book I Fugue ♪ᵧ♪ᵧ♪ and in the Prelude in Book II as ᵧ♪ᵧ♪ᵧ♬ appears here, but only once, as ♩ᵧ♩ᵧ|♩ in bar 33. In other words, the mood of this Fugue has evolved from those depicted in the other pieces and has now become one of introspective reflection.

In the final section, with inimitable skill, Bach brings the two main themes of opposing emotional connotations into perfect balance, and in doing so creates a consummate musical expression of one of life's deepest truths. Joy and sorrow constitute the very fabric of human existence. There cannot be the one without the other.

19

A Major

PRELUDE A major I

FUGUE A major I

PRELUDE A major II

A major is recognized as a Trinity key, and the spiritual significance of the number 3 is expressed in various way in pieces in this tonality. Bach did not write extensively in A major, but the works he gave us are of great beauty, brilliant craftsmanship and striking originality, with a wide range of emotional content. Many choral works in this key reflect an abiding faith in heavenly compassion and blessings, but interestingly, a few express wrath and indignation.

The latter is found twice in the *St. John Passion*: the bitter taunting of Peter, "*Bist du nicht* (Art thou not) in chorus 17, and in the even more vehement *Weg, weg, mit dem ... Kreuzige ihn* (Away, away with him ... crucify him) in chorus 44. In the aria *Rase nur verwegner Schwarm*, bass soloist rages at the enemies of August III in Cantata BWV 215, *Preise dein Glücke*.

The former is movingly expressed in Motet BWV 228, *Fürchte dich nicht, ich bin bei dir* (Fear not, I am with thee), and in two sublime soprano arias: *Ich bin schön* (I am splendid, I am fair) from Cantata BWV 49 in which the melody is strikingly similar to that of the Prelude in A in Book I; and *Gottes Engel weichen nie* (God's angels never fail) from Cantata BWV 149.

Instrumental compositions in this key include Preludes and Fugues in the *WTC*; Invention 12, Sinfonia 12, English Suite no. 1, a harpsichord Concerto, a Sonata for clavier and violin, a Suite for clavier and violin, and an organ Prelude and Fugue.

Prelude, A Major, Book I

Three contrasting melodies, each with its own symbolic references, are combined in this Prelude. The first has the characteristics of a dance with light, lilting rhythm, a leap of the sixth (a consistent joy symbol for Bach) and a rapid rising and falling melody which is identified as a "flight of angels"—a symbol established in the Chorale Prelude BWV 607 *Vom Himmel kam die Engel Schar* (From Heaven came a group of angels) and in the first of the Canonic Variations BWV 769 on the hymn *Vom Himmel hoch da komm' ich her* (From high Heaven I come here). The second is the descending chromatic scale, historically representing pain and anguish. The third is a syncopated sigh motif—sighs of weariness and longing. Bach also emphasizes the sigh in a series of descending steps.

Bach was very conscious of the affect of opposing themes in contrary motion. A revealing example can be found in a canon he wrote in a friend's autograph book in 1747. The melodies are:

Beneath the music he has written *Symbolum—Christus Coronabit Crucigeros* (Christ will crown the Cross-bearers). It is a promise that sorrow will be transformed to happiness. It seems clear that this sentiment is intentionally expressed in this Prelude.

A modulation to F-sharp minor at bar 12 is especially poignant with a partial inversion of the first theme, which affects its character. The melody now has a diminished third intensifying the melancholy produced by the inversion and minor key.

In the first chorus (in A major) of Cantata BWV 3 *Ach Gott, wie manches Herzeleid*, Bach has given the violins the sigh motif in the two forms found in this Prelude:

The words of the chorus embody the subject of the Cantata: "Ah God, how much sorrow / meets me at this time / the narrow way is full of sadness /

on which I must travel to heaven." In the third aria the bass sings first a grief motif which quickly changes to a joy motif. Throughout the Cantata is reassurance that pain will be followed by joy.

This reassurance is depicted in the final bars of the Prelude. The darker motifs have disappeared. The soprano soars "heavenward," released from the other voices which fall back to Earth.

Fugue, A Major, Book I

With its heraldic opening note, unique in the whole *WTC*, this unconventional and innovative Fugue is in a class by itself. Something wonderful is sure to unfold.

In Czerny's edition of the *WTC* he added many interpretive details, which, it is assumed, relate directly to how Beethoven played these works. He places a fortissimo on the first note. It is not hard to imagine the electrifying effect Beethoven would create. With that one note attention must be caught as if in a moment of suspense and held through the rests.

The melody of the subject ascends in strides of intervals of the fourth—that fundamental religious symbol always associated with the Trinity. So eager is the second voice to enter it does not wait until the completion of the subject, but answers midway, and at a specific moment—the seventh note of the subject, the number that, for Bach, symbolizes the Holy Spirit.

Bach cadences the subject in a variety of ways. One is of particular interest. At bars 4–5 and 7–8 the melody falls a major seventh. (There are also two instances in the Prelude where this specific interval occurs—the bass melody in bars 15 and16.) The significance of this striking interval is illustrated in the glorious aria *Mein gläubiges Herze* (My faithful heart, rejoice) from Cantata BWV 68. The soprano affirms her certainty in the leap down of a major seventh on the last two words of the phrase *dein Jesus ist da* (thy Jesus is here). (See C-sharp major Fugue Book I for a quote of this melody.)

At bar 23 the subject is joined by a flowing, graceful melody—the angels of the Prelude are again present. Joy and elation now increase to the point where the strides of intervals of the fourth in the subject burst forth into leaps of the sixth.

In bar 46, at the approach to the final exuberant statements of the transformed subject, another drop of the major seventh rings out in the bass—its affirmation as strong as that created in the soprano aria.

In this powerful Fugue confidence and trust in the fulfillment of the promise of relief from burden and sorrow, implied in the Prelude, is magnified.

Prelude, A Major, Book II

At the end of the Fugue in A major Book I, Bach left us full of joyful anticipation. Now, in this Prelude he surely brings us into the company of angels.

The serene, pastoral melody begins over an important holy symbol in the bass—the descending octave. This is the Sanctus symbol (*B minor Mass*) which appears in Bach's music not only in an open octave but also in a broken four-note-form chord, as we find here. (See the bass of the beginning of the A-flat major Prelude Book II for another variant.) Two revealing instances can be found where this form of the Sanctus symbol is sung by Jesus: in recitative no. 28 in the *St. John Passion, Du sagst's, ich bin ein König* (Thou say'st, I am a king) and in recitative no. 24 in the *St. Matthew Passion, Setzet euch hie* (Sit ye here).

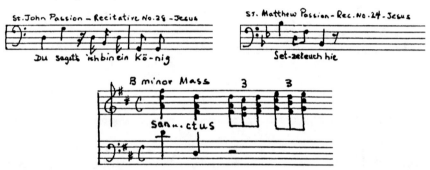

Within this Prelude, in keeping with the Trinity theme, the open octave motif is found three times.

In Cantata BWV 190, *Singet dem Herrn ein neues Lied* (Sing to the Lord a new song) the dance-like rhythm in triple meter of the A major alto solo *Lobe Zion deinen Gott* inspired W. Murray Young to comment, "The peacefully lilting music seems to give an image of the tranquil meadows of heaven" (*The Cantatas of J.S. Bach—An Analytical Guide*, p. 61). Did Bach intend to recapture the mood of that aria from his 1724 Cantata when he composed this Prelude in the same key?

With inimitable skill Bach weaves his celestial melody, with its inversion, choosing two places to include a rhythmic joy motif among the flowing triplets (bars 9 and 21).

The dominant ascending character of the music throughout the Prelude is gloriously depicted in the final bars as the melody soars above the third Sanctus symbol.

Fugue, A Major, Book II

Gentle and peaceful in mood, simple in design, the charm of this Fugue lies in its graceful melodies and lilting dotted rhythm.

The subject contains 19 notes—the first section of 9 and the last of 10. Remembering that this is a Trinity key, it is inevitable that Bach would integrate the number 3 (here in multiple) in this last piece. But the number 10 is not without significance. It is Bach's reference to the Ten Commandments. A specific example is the Chorale Prelude BWV 678 *Dies sind die heil'-gen Zehn Gebot'* (These are the holy Ten Commandments) where the pedal part states the theme 10 times. In this Fugue, not only is that number part of the subject but the subject itself appears 10 times.

In the opening of the theme there is a melodic pattern that echoes part of the melody of the A major Prelude Book I.

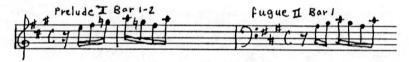

At bar 19 a single note, F-sharp, in the soprano is placed in relief—appearing in kinship with the A major Fugue Book I but of a very different character from that Fugue's signal note.

Not only is the open octave figure carried forward from the companion Prelude, but an even more decisive bond between the two pieces is established in the beautiful chromatic modulation passage that occurs at exactly the same bars, 17–18.

The combination of two joy motifs ♫♩ ♫♩ and ♫♫ ♫♫ that Bach has included here has a counterpart in the Sinfonia in the same key.

The motif pattern highlights the joyfulness inherent in Bach's A major music. It is as wonderful here as it is in the Sinfonia.

Within the simplicity of his design, Bach, the master, has woven parts of all the other pieces into this last piece in the A major group. The abiding sentiment supremely unified.

20

A Minor

PRELUDE A minor I

FUGUE A minor I

PRELUDE A minor II

A spirit of confidence and strength, resolute amidst adversity, characterizes many of Bach's compositions in the key of A minor. These attributes are often reinforced by a propelling rhythmic energy and specific motivic language. Such emotional dimensions are integral to the Preludes and Fugues in A minor in the WTC.

The repertoire in this key abounds in superb instrumental and choral compositions. Among the former are Invention no. 13, Sinfonia no. 13, a Concerto for four claviers, Partita no. 3, English Suite no. 2, an organ Concerto (after Vivaldi), the organ Prelude and Fugue BWV 543 (The Great), a violin Concerto, a Sonata for unaccompanied violin, and a Concerto for clavier, flute and violin.

Among the choral works, five examples define relevant aspects Bach associated with this tonality: In the *St. Matthew Passion* the tenor aria *Geduld! Geduld!* (Patience! Patience!) and the soprano aria *Aus Liebe will mein Heiland sterben* (For love will my Saviour die)—confidence and faith; the chorus *Wir dürfen niemand töten* (For us all killing is unlawful) in the *St. John Passion*; the first chorus of Cantata 126 *Erhalt' uns, Herr, bei deinem Wort* (Keep us, Lord, in Thy word)—victory over enemies both temporal and spiritual; in Cantata 70, the alto aria *Wann kommt der Tag* (When will the day come)—an admonition to wake up before destruction befalls us.

Prelude, A Minor, Book I

The dance form of this Prelude serves primarily to give rhythmic impetus to the music's underlying mood of unrest and turmoil, which will fully erupt in its companion Fugue.

This mood is established immediately with the theme progressing directly from the tonic key to two harmonically rising imitations pointedly altered by a diminished seventh chord—that historical symbol of pain and anxiety. The modulation to the dominant key is marked by two dissonant intervals of equally disturbing implication—the tritone (the Diabolus in musica) and the major seventh. The E minor statement of the theme, in keeping with its inherent association as a Passion key, is intensified by solid chords and melodic elaboration. That there are three chords may not be incidental, the number 3 being symbolic of the Trinity.

From this emotionally charged atmosphere, Bach, again by way of a tritone in bar 8, begins a highly significant modulatory sequence during which the diminished seventh is not heard in the thematic bass line, the three chords are all concords, and the soprano melody makes a dramatic approach to that most affirmative of all keys—C major. Bach brings a special sonority to the theme in this tonality with a deep tonic pedal note as a third voice.

In the cadence of this C major passage, and in preparation for the modulation to G minor, a melody, not irrelevant to the mood of the Prelude, appears in the inner voice. This melody is the dominant theme in the tenor of the organ Chorale Prelude BWV 617 *Herr Gott, nun schleuss den Himmel auf* (Lord God, now unlock Heaven), which Schweitzer (*J.S. Bach*) describes as "sorrowful longing."

Once again using a tritone in the bass, Bach moves directly from the C major cadence to the diminished seventh of G minor, throbbing with a repeated leading note. With a descending leap of a major seventh, the Chorale theme now appears in G minor, and it too moves by way of a tritone in the bass to the diminished seventh of D minor. Another descending leap of a major seventh accentuates the theme's D minor statement from which will evolve two climactic moments. The first is attacked head-on with a piercing major seventh leap up to G-sharp and concludes with a pointed fall of an augmented fifth. The second, apexing on a high A, precipitates a spiraling descent, plummeting to an emotional nadir two octaves below. But Bach now signifies a powerful symbolic transition. Like the phoenix rising from the ashes, the music, above a resonant tonic pedal point, soars in spiritual triumph to a five-voice major cadence.

Fugue, A Minor, Book I

It was thumbs-down for this Fugue in the opinion of the two early chroniclers of Bach and his music. Forkel included it among those in the first book he deemed "imperfect." Spitta (*J.S. Bach*) thought it "pedantic and lacking in imagination." Part of their criticism perhaps lies in the nature of the subject with its anapest rhythm, which they may have felt becomes monotonous in its seemingly interminable repetition. But, as subsequent scholars and performers have revealed, the unrelenting anapest rhythm *is* what the affect of the piece is all about. It is the formidable force in defining the character of the Fugue.

To be sure, it is a long and difficult Fugue and demands considerable ingenuity and skill to shape the architecture, plan dynamic contrasts, and develop and sustain emotional tension through to the powerful finale.

In discussing the G-sharp minor Fugue in Book I, I suggested, in view of the nature of the subject and the overall tone of the piece, that it may have been composed while Bach was unjustly confined to jail in Weimar in 1717, when, from contemporary evidence, it is believed he did considerable work on the first book of the WTC. This Fugue may also have originated during that stressful experience, so infused is the music with a spirit of righteous indignation, determination and confidence. Augmenting the effect of the anapest rhythm in the opening statement is the emphatic melodic fall of a diminished seventh, the symbol of pain. It, along with dissonant major and minor sevenths that appear in inversions of the theme, constitute a pivotal element in the language of both the Fugue and its companion Prelude.

Bach completes the theme with a strong melody. Not only does it close with an resolute interval of a fourth (a fundamental religious symbol) and a perfect fifth, but, of equal significance, this melody consists of 14 notes, the symbolic number which represents his name—B-flat-2, A-1, C-3, B-natural (H)-8 = 14. Bach encoded this number in various ways throughout his music. It became a kind of personal signature or identification.

Although there is no regular countersubject, as is often the case where stretto and inversion are a major part of the design, in the exposition Bach has placed a descending scale melody (taken from the subject) in counterpoint with each of the subject entries. It is a simple motif, but often in choral works, in particular the Credo in the B minor Mass, measured strong steps symbolize strength and confident faith.

Credo – B-minor Mass

As such, the motif emphasizes the character of the subject itself. In the fourth entry, Bach further augments its importance and meaning by doubling it in thirds. It is a powerful exposition and establishes the very foundation of the emotional dimension he will develop.

At the end of the exposition Bach introduces the inversion of the subject. Its entry is specially marked by appearing in the 14th bar. The theme in this form takes on a subtle change in character. In contrast to the aggressive tone of the subject, the inverted melody seems to sublimate the anger, and transform it to a deeper level. The original drop of the diminished seventh now becomes a rise of a major seventh, plaintive and beseeching.

The more temperate mood of this melody is also discerned in the first statement by a beautiful modulation to G major, the cadence delicately ornamented. Moving through C major and poignant D minor, the gradual modulation to A minor and return to the main theme is intensified with two marvelous chords of the 13th in bar 24, and a predominance of double thirds in the bass line.

The return of the subject in bar 27 marks the next important phase in the development. In bar 28 (a multiple of 14) the first appearance of stretto begins. Bach devotes the next 13 bars solely to stretto of the main theme, then inserts a short episodic "reprieve" of tension at bar 40 before continuing on to a strong affirmative modulation and cadence in C major at bar 48.

Now it is the inversion's turn. Again, Bach devotes the next 13 bars solely to stretto of this theme. And again, he inserts a short episode above a pedal dominant note before continuing—this time to a decisive cadence in D minor (bar 64).

The next section brings the subject and inversion closer together, each in stretto. In fact, the first stretto between the two themes is heard in this section. In bar 67 the inverted theme begins just before the end of the 14th entry of the subject.

Another short episode serves as a transition to and a preparation for a fervent confrontation between the two themes, during which the 14th entry of the inverted theme is accentuated by a dissonant leap of a ninth in the voice above it, then cut short by the main theme entering abruptly in stretto. The tension inevitably leads to a dramatic climax on the fermata. But it is the main theme that then asserts its supremacy. It is a statement of uncompromising conviction.

The coda presents a technical problem. It cannot be played as written without the use of a pedal keyboard. Bach owned a pedal attachment for a clavichord for which this piece may have been intended. Two solutions are possible—a page turner plays the pedal note at the beginning of each bar, or the player can anticipate the downbeat chords by restriking the pedal note. Do whatever works to capture the grandeur of the glorious finale. It is a moving, triumphant union of the two themes, made transcendent at the close with the opening notes of each theme in double thirds and a major plagal cadence. Resolute and indomitable.

Prelude, A Minor, Book II

Bach, ever conscious of the challenges of adversity in human lives, moves from the distress and inner turbulence faced confidently, and even heroically, in the A minor Prelude and Fugue in the first book, to a still deeper level of conflict and despair in the Prelude and Fugue in the second book.

Like the Prelude in the first book, this Prelude is also in a dance form, an allemande, but unlike the former, is strictly a two-part Invention. The interrelationship of the two voices is vital and consequential in creating the extreme emotional dimension of the thematic material.

Bach uses here three of the most potent motifs in the lexicon of symbolic musical language.

The descending chromatic scale has always been a symbol of grief and sorrow. It is heard in this context throughout Bach's choral works. The definitive example of the import of this motif is in the *Crucifixus* of the B minor Mass, where it appears 13 times.

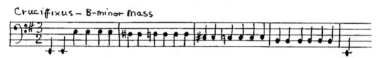

Of equal tragic and grief-stricken implications is its role in this Prelude. Both the theme and its accompanying bass melody descend chromatically. The dolor of the bass can be increased by two-note slurs, Bach's sigh motif synonymous with tears.

Adding to the darkness is the tritone (the Diabolus in musica), an interval denoting fear and even, at times, terror. It is heard throughout the piece— in the theme melody, its inversion, and some of the bridge sections. This interval is also a vital element in the A minor Prelude in the first book, one of several links Bach makes between the two sets of pieces in this key.

The third motif is the ascending chromatic scale formed in the inversion of the theme in the second part of the Prelude. It is associated with heightened anxiety and painful longing for deliverance from despair. This is dramatically expressed in the magnificent fifth chorus *Israel hoffe auf den Herrn* of Cantata 131 *Aus der Tiefe rufe ich, Herr, zu dir* (Out of the depths I cry, Lord, to Thee). Hope for God's mercy and redemption.

Following the chromaticism and tritones in the theme, Bach completes the melody with a most telling rhythmic motif—step-wise syncopation, which in his choral works often denoted exhaustion and uncertainty.

But now let us look at the bridge or episodic sections, for within them are intimations of strength, glimmers of hope, albeit tenuous. Of particular interest in these passages is the appearance of the anapest rhythm ♪♪♩, which Bach has carried forward from the Fugue in the first book (♩♫). Moreover, it is heard melodically, with few exceptions, exactly as it did in the theme of the Fugue—as a mordent. In its new context it undergoes a kind of transmutation, no longer aggressive and confrontational but bordering on a joy motif. Notice too that the harmonic direction in bar 3 is upward, with strong ascending steps in the bass. Each of these episodes has its own beauty, but none equal the pathos of the one which precedes the final entries of the subject, especially the throbbing repeated notes in the bass and turns in the melody. If we look back at the earlier Fugue we see those turns in the first section of its subject theme.

One last symbolic figure to mention is the fall of an octave—recognized as the Sanctus symbol (from the *B minor Mass*). Of course, not all drops of an octave represent this symbol. It depends on its figuration in the context of a composition. That it can be interpreted as a Sanctus symbol within the affect of this Fugue seems plausible. It occurs several times in the piece, most notably at the seventh (the holy number) entry of the subject at bar 11, the end of the first section and beginning of the second, twice during the last episode, and as the final bass notes of the composition.

The significance of its inclusion within a depiction of extreme sorrow cannot be underestimated. It reflects the absolute spiritual trust which guided Bach throughout his life.

No one has described this deeply affecting Prelude more beautifully than Wilfrid Mellers when he wrote, "it renders incarnate in sound, not one man's distress at a particular time and place, but *lacrimae rerum*, universalized through the crucible of Bach's imagination" (*Bach and the Dance of God*, p. 55).

Fugue, A Minor, Book II

If, in the Fugue in this key in the first book, Bach's depiction of a soul in great turmoil and distress seemed almost unbearably acute, we can scarcely fathom the degree of anguish and anger pouring forth from his Fugue in the second book. Indeed, Bodky (*Interpretation*) described it as "one of the most explosive pieces ever written by Bach." The depth of pain and sorrow expressed in its companion Prelude should have prepared us. It was surely a premonition.

The affect of the piece is explicit in the subject. First and foremost, the opening four-note melody forms the historic cross motif. It is the ultimate symbol of pain and suffering.

Not only does Bach begin the subject with this motif, he concludes it by forming it again in the final four-note melody (a kind of diminution) and specifically marking these notes with strokes. These strokes do not denote a staccatissimo as they would in Haydn or Mozart, but marcato, heavily accented detached notes. So powerful is this initial statement of the cross motif, it continues to reverberate in the connecting melody to the counter-subject (note the biting descent of the major seventh) and in the counter-subject itself.

It is the absolute core of the Fugue. There is scarcely a bar that does not contain it in at least one of the voices.

The cross motif is, of course, detected visually. The melody which forms the motif must inevitably imprint the symbol aurally. Bach does this dra-matically in the opening notes of the subject by adding relevant symbol-ism—the rising interval of the fourth (a fundamental religious symbol) and an exposed falling diminished seventh (always a symbol of pain). It is note-worthy to mention here that Handel began the chorus *And with His Stripes* in the *Messiah* with this same melodic motif, as did Mozart for the *Kyrie* in his *Requiem*.

The countersubject, with searing scales, anapest rhythm, syncopation, and seething trill translates the symbolism of the cross into concrete terms. Not only does it evoke a sense of rage, but also a pictorial image of the soul staggering under an immense burden.

Rather than displaying any special contrapuntal devices, Bach focuses entirely on imprinting on our minds the powerful spiritual and emotional implications of the theme.

Let us look at some special details and moments in the unfolding of this extraordinary Fugue. The trill is always heard in conjunction with the second part of the theme, intensifying and amplifying the vehement mood.

Number symbolism also plays an important role. Of the eight entries of the subject, Bach has so designed it that the subject (Dux) appears three times—the symbolic number for the Trinity and therefore of spiritual con-notation, and the answer (Comes) five times—the number symbol for the crucifixion (the five wounds inflicted on Jesus). Furthermore, the fifth entry of the theme (bar 13), which is at the same time the third appearance of the Comes, piercingly erupts from a sweeping scale to the highest pitch of all the entries, and indeed, to the highest note in the composition. It is also highly significant that this passage is in the key of E minor, the Passion key.

Since the symbolic numbers 3 and 5 have received representation in Bach's design, it is not unexpected that he would include the number 7, the holiest of holy symbols, not only of biblical origin but, even in alchemical theory, symbolic as the gateway between Earth and heaven. He gives very special treatment to the seventh entry of the subject (Dux). It begins in the 21st bar (three times seven) and under the first section of the theme, the turbulence of the countersubject is augmented by embellishment.

Through all the pieces in A minor Bach has consistently carried for-ward specific motivic and symbolic material—the tritone, the falling dimin-ished seventh, trenchant leaps of major and minor sevenths, ninths and tenths, passages of double thirds, and the anapest rhythm. Not only do they define the character of each piece, but they are vital elements in building the emotional dimension of the theme of anguish, sorrow and turmoil in progressive stages to its most intense and ultimate degree in the last of the group.

It is from the Preludes, though, that Bach draws to this Fugue two the-matic figurations that prove of tremendous consequence. The rising and descending scale patterns of the theme and its inversion from the compan-ion Prelude become explosive motifs under the cross motif in the episodes. And in a remarkable passage in the approach to the end of the Fugue, Bach goes back to the closing moments in the first Prelude, re-creating its spiral-ing descending scale patterns, this time plummeting two and a half octaves. Number symbolism is ingrained in this cataclysmic image—five scales crash down on the fifth entry of the Comes, the eighth and last statement of the subject.

Beethoven, the moment before he died, raised his head and shook his fist in defiance at the thunderclap. Is Bach not also symbolizing the same spirit with thundering trills, accented anapest rhythm and dark minor cadence as he ends this momentous Fugue?

21

B-Flat Major

Bb major PRELUDE-I

FUGUE Bb major-I

Prelude-Bb major.II

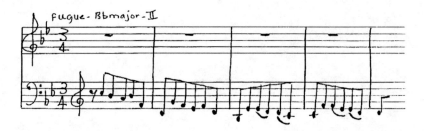

In contrast to an abundance of choruses and arias in B-flat major, Bach wrote only eight instrumental compositions in this key. All, with one exception, are for clavier. In addition to the four pieces in the WTC they are Invention no. 14, Sinfonia no. 14, Partita no. 1, and Brandenburg Concerto no. 6. Each one a gem, uniquely revealing the special qualities of this tonality.

Three exceptionally beautiful arias in this key exemplify the moods and sentiments most relevant to the instrumental music: the soprano aria *Ich folge dir gleichfalls mit freudigen Schritten* (I follow Thee also with joy-lightened footsteps) in the *St. John Passion*; the bass aria *Mache dich, mein Herze rein* (Make thee clean, my heart) in the *St. Matthew Passion*; and the soprano aria *Himmlische Vergnügsamkeit* (Heavenly contentment) in the secular Cantata no. 204 (1728)—a special cantata which Bach may have written for Anna Magdalena in which she sings of contentment with her life.

Prelude, B-Flat Major, Book I

Familiarity with Bach's organ Toccatas is an advantage in forming a conception of the style of performance for this brilliant Prelude. It is a real little Toccata and has many characteristics of the larger organ works. Its sole aim is to display the virtuosic skill of the performer, to dazzle the listener and, as was undoubtedly the case with the organ works, to reveal and revel in the rich sonorities of the instrument.

The broken chord was an important development in music, greatly enhancing harmonic language and presenting infinite possibilities to a composer as well as new technical challenges to a performer. Bach's unparalleled mastery of this figure is amply displayed throughout the WTC. His imagination knew no bounds.

The broken form he chose for this Prelude is one he had not used before in Book I. The simplicity of its figuration is perfect for the affect Bach intended. Not only does it afford a melodic line in the top notes but also, with rapid harmonic progressions, creates dynamic rhythmic energy and excitement. Bach used a similar figuration of the chord in the Giga of the B-flat Partita, and for much the same purpose—a minimum of notes for maximum exuberance.

In the second section Bach increases the dynamics with a more elaborate form of the chord, for this is where the music will reach dramatic heights with resounding solid chords in dotted French rhythm and electrifying scale cascades. The climax in bar 17 rises in arpeggio to the highest note in the piece and subsides onto glorious chords, so expressive with melodic inner voices.

A most important character of all Toccatas is the spirit of improvisation. Spontaneous rhythmic freedom is essential. Creative imagination is the key to an exciting performance of this Prelude. And don't miss the humor in the final bar.

Fugue, B-Flat Major, Book I

Bach follows the Prelude with a Fugue equally exuberant, sparkling with wit and humor. The fun starts right off in the subject, with the rhythm of a peasant dance, leaps of an interval so often appearing in joyful contexts in Bach's music—the major 6th, and merry passages of 16ths that extend the melody to create the longest of all his fugal subjects in the WTC—38 notes!

This theme is set in triple counterpoint with two countersubjects, each contributing to the gaiety of the scenario. The repeated note figure of the first countersubject brings to mind the melody of the first duet—*Mer hahn en neue Oberkeet* (We have a new overlord) in the Peasant Cantata. The soprano and bass tell us that their new master has invited everyone to enjoy free beer at the tavern in celebration of his acquisition of an estate.

The second countersubject is described by Keller (*Well-Tempered Clavier*) as "short impertinent interjections." Bach suggests its mischievous character by presenting the first motif in four variations and the second motif as a saucy imitation of part of the main theme.

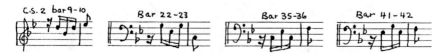

Except for its joyful spirit, there is only the briefest thematic connection in the Fugue to its companion Prelude. In both episodes the inversion
of the first motif of the subject forms a sequential pattern. If you look closely
at bars 19–20 you will see hidden in this first appearance of the inverted
motif the melody of the top notes of the broken chords heard at the beginning of the Prelude.

Humor and wit are part and parcel of Bach's whole design of the Fugue.
He is smiling at every twist and turn. He puts a redundant subject entry in
the exposition and a false entry just before he starts the final section. Even
the theme, as it opens the piece, is never heard again starting on the dominant note. The final section begins in E-flat major and the last entry also
begins on the subdominant—arriving "home" on B-flat major just in time
for the coda. The Peasant Cantata theme of the first countersubject and the
little figure from the subject with its imitation from the second countersubject dance their way to the closing bars.

Prelude, B-Flat Major, Book II

The spirit of joyfulness continues in the B-flat major pieces in the second book, but Bach now turns from the earthly character expressed in this
key in the first book to one more spiritual in nature.

The Prelude is written in a highly developed early sonata form. It is
also in dance form in two sections, of which there are no fewer than 10 in
the second book. In contrast to the peasant celebration of the Fugue in
Book I, this is a dance in heavenly spheres. The pastoral character of the
music creates an aura of serene and peaceful happiness. Bach chose the key
of B-flat major for one of the loveliest pastoral scenes in his choral works—
the soprano aria *Schafe können sicher weiden* (Sheep may safely graze) from
Cantata 208, the Hunting Cantata.

Rising and falling waves of scale patterns forming a dominant feature in
a composition have been identified as Bach's tone picture of the appearance
of angels. The identification comes particularly from the organ chorales *Vom*

Himmel hoch, da komm' ich her (From heaven on high I come here) and *Vom Himmel kam der Engel Schar* (From heaven came the host of angels). Here, too, flowing ascending and descending scales form the essence of the composition which, in turn, has prompted the description the "Flight of Angels" Prelude.

Bach seems mainly to have reserved the sections in three voices to symbolize an "angelic presence." It is there, accompanied by rhythmic dance figures, that the scales flow from voice to voice, as though constantly moving between heaven and Earth.

These angelic moments are connected by passages predominantly in two voices where the contrapuntal writing is notable in both visual and tonal beauty. Melodies in stretto and parallel and contrary motion flow effortlessly through extraordinary harmonic progressions, the most affecting being where Bach has used the Neapolitan sixth—the G-flat approaching the F major cadence at the end of the first section, the A-flat in the approach to G major in the second bar of the second section, and the climactic C-flat in the modulation to the tonic key in the final bars.

Of special charm are the two crossed-hands passages. In discussing the Prelude in the first book, I suggested an affinity between it and the Giga in the B-flat Partita in the form of broken chord. Is it not intriguing that Bach should choose another figure from that Giga as part of his design for the B-flat Prelude in the second book? It is true that in both cases the crossed-hands notes are the harmonic basis, but the affect of each piece is quite different. The question here is, should the dotted notes be played detached and crisply, or does a sustained tone enhance the particular affect of this piece?

The conclusion of the development in the second section evokes a sublime vision of heavenly grace descending on the pastoral scene, pausing in a hushed suspension on the dominant.

The coda ushers in a pictorial shift with music that surely depicts the now heavenward flight of angels, surging in undulating scales and culminating in a beatific climax. All is peace and joy in the closing cadence.

Fugue, B-Flat Major, Book II

The peaceful mood in which the Prelude closed evolves into another dimension in its companion Fugue. It is as though the angelic presence intimated in the Prelude gave only fleeting glimpses of heavenly peace and joy and has caused the soul to yearn all the more for release from life's conflicts and uncertainties. The thematic material which Bach chose for the Fugue and which permeates the whole composition is clearly designed to depict this deeply human sentiment.

Bach made a subtle connection between the closing bar of the Prelude and the opening of the Fugue's subject. The descending B-flat broken chord becomes part of the subject's melody. Another element in common with the Prelude is the weaving and flowing of melodies in parallel and contrary motion.

The subject consists of 24 notes and is divided into two equal parts. The number 12 has spiritual connotations in that it is a symbol in Bach's music of the Creator and of faith. Also prominent in the theme is the interval of the fourth—always a fundamental religious symbol. We shall see too that the number 3, the symbol for the Trinity, has its place in Bach's design.

The motif in the first section of the subject, based on the turn, lovely in its gracefulness, is one that Bach used earlier in a context which perhaps sheds light on its significance in this Fugue. It is heard in the tenor part of the organ Chorale Prelude BWV 617 *Herr Gott, nun schleuss den Himmel auf* (Lord God, now unlock Heaven), which Schweitzer (*J.S. Bach*) describes as "a sorrowful longing."

One might also contemplate the symbolic implication of the turn and its use in connection with the word *unlock*. An affinity of sentiment between the Chorale Prelude and this Fugue seems certain to lie in this melodic motif. Its important role in the emotional dimension of the Fugue is underlined by its constant presence—it appears no fewer than 46 times.

The melodies in the second part of the subject consist entirely of a series of sigh motifs, the slurs specifically written on the score by Bach himself.

This appoggiatura figure in his music is synonymous with tears. In the bass aria from the *St. Matthew Passion* mentioned at the beginning of this chapter, this figure is a vital element in the orchestral accompaniment. The theme of the aria is a longing for inner peace.

Although there is no real countersubject established in the exposition, at the start of the second section of the Fugue two quasi-countersubjects are introduced with the subject.

This is where the symbolic number 3 comes into play—three long step-wise notes in the first one and three sequences of a three-note rhythmic pattern in the second. This happens at bar 33. Both these motivic themes rise melodically in contrast to the falling melodies of the subject, and it is from this point that Bach begins to build emotional tension through the development section. An acute moment is symbolized by the huge leap of a 15th, which erupts from the dissonant, unresolved C in bar 40, at the 6th subject entry. The emotional dimension gains momentum with harmonic progressions that move through G minor, E-flat major, F minor to C minor. Of particular significance is the passage through E-flat major (the Trinity key), marked by a series of parallel double third intervals. In the Middle Ages this interval was considered dissonant, but in the Renaissance it became, especially in a passage of parallel thirds, as Wilfrid Mellers so eloquently describes, "an incarnation of sensuous bliss" (*Bach and the Dance of God*, p. 40).

From the consciousness of certitude felt in the E-flat tonality, Bach gently moves downward through minor keys, culminating in a very moving passage where the heretofore melodically rising second countersubject now descends with the theme motifs in a long sequential series. At its cadence in F major, the soprano leaps a 9th, an interval always associated with emotional intensity, to begin the 10th and final entrance of the subject.

The coda begins with the second countersubject motif thrice rising above the subject motifs, supported by the three-note first countersubject. The approach to the final cadence is one of Bach's loveliest and most poignant passages. The insertion of the little rhythmic motif ♪♫♩ is one of the master's magical touches. It is a rhythmic figure which imbues the aria in this key *Schafe können sicher weiden* (Sheep may safely graze) with its peaceful ambience, and surely meaningfully chosen to appear here just before the climax. For despite the sorrow implied by the diminished chord and the descending chromatic bass line, there is an ineffable sense of peace in the closing cadence of this 93 (a multiple of three) bar Fugue.

22

B-Flat Minor

The keys that Bach introduced to music literature, those of five, six and seven sharps and flats, are all represented by works of exceptional beauty and power.

Although there are no other instrumental compositions in B-flat minor, it is worth noting that Bach chose this key for the Chorale O *hilf, Christe, Gottes Sohn* (Help, O Jesus, God's own Son) which appears just before the recitative that leads into the final chorus of the *St. John Passion*. Even more significantly, it is the key of the deeply moving *Eli, Eli, lama, lama asabthani?* (My God, My God, why hast Thou forsaken me?), Jesus' last words from the Cross, in the *St. Matthew Passion*.

The grief and anguish expressed in these two numbers from choral works pervade the Preludes and Fugues in B-flat minor.

Prelude, B-Flat Minor, Book I

The sense of mourning which permeates this Prelude, with its solemn, measured pace, invokes an image of a funeral procession. The emotional impact of the music lies not only in the melody but also in the continuous tension of dissonance and the release of resolution.

Bach was passionately intent on discovering the secrets of harmony, which he was sure reflected the wisdom of Nature. Perfection and reality lie beyond the physical world but can be grasped intuitively. The artist attempts to reveal these ideals on the physical plane. Christoph Wolff (*Bach: Essays on his Life and Music*) suggests that Bach may have been familiar with the teachings of Plotinus, which included the nature of beauty and perfection.

Although it is unlikely that Bach spent any time philosophizing about his art (theories and treatises on music held little interest for him), there is no doubt that he contemplated the mystical power of music and its effect on the soul. This Prelude, through Bach's mastery and intuitive genius, is a manifestation of the power of harmony.

The repeated pedal bass note in the first two bars portends the emotional tone of the piece. There are many instances where Bach uses this device when depicting sorrow or spiritual darkness: the opening choruses of both Passions; the soprano recitative *Wiewohl mein Herz in Tränen schwimmt* (Although my heart swims in tears) and the tenor aria *O Schmerz! Hier zittert das gequälte Herz!* (O pain! Here trembles the troubled heart!) in the *St. Matthew Passion*. We find it also at the beginning of the Preludes in D minor and G minor in Book I.

The constant repetition of the two rhythms ♪♫♫♫♫♪ and ♫♫♫♫ increases the overwhelming effect as the music progresses. Although the second pattern is more often heard as a joy motif, Bach also gave it a somber and threatening character. In the chorus *Kreuzige* (Crucify)

in the *St. John Passion*, this rhythm drives relentlessly to reach dramatic levels. The organ Chorale Prelude BWV 718 *Christ lag in Todesbanden* (Christ lay in death's dark tomb) begins with a bass melody in this rhythmic pattern which descends to "dark depths."

With skillful tonal emphasis, the beauty of the interweaving melodic themes as they pass from voice to voice is imprinted on our consciousness. It is a supreme example of harmonic polyphony.

No one can be unaffected by the sublimity of the passage that begins at bar 13, with its beautiful transparent texture and harmony free of the stress of dissonance. How gently Bach leads us down from the empyreal heights of the soprano melody to the cadence at bar 20. Now he will build the heart-rending climax.

Three elements contribute to the powerful impact of this climax: the contrary motion in double thirds in the outermost voices (Bach returns to this double third figure for the same purpose at the end of the B-flat minor Fugue in Book II); an increase to nine voices for the diminished seventh chord; the placing of a fermata over this chord, a symbol not often found in the keyboard works but purposefully chosen at moments of emotional impasse. A very revealing example of Bach's placement of a fermata is in the soprano aria *Aus Liebe will mein Heiland sterben* (For love will my Saviour die) in the St. Matthew Passion. It is indicated at each of the three times she sings the word *sterben* (die). (See the F-sharp minor chapter, the Prelude in Book II, where the melody is illustrated.)

Following this climactic moment, Bach imparts a feeling of renewed strength as the key now turns toward the B flat major final chord. Yet the melodic theme in the tenor with its G-flat tells us that sorrow still lingers.

Fugue, B-Flat Minor, Book I

It is significant that Bach chose a five-part Fugue, of which there are only two in the *WTC*, as a companion to the multivoiced, richly harmonized Prelude. The mood of the Prelude is unmistakably carried forward in the Fugue, vocal in character, solemn in tempo, and consummate in contrapuntal skill. We cannot help but marvel at the subtle emotional effect Bach creates with the gradual progressions from three voices, then four, to that decisive moment, the appearance of all five voices.

The subject opens with a mournful descending fourth (another correspondence with the F-Sharp minor Prelude in Book II), a cry made all the more plaintive by a rest—a gasp of breath before leaping a minor ninth for the last four notes of this tragic theme. A melody which rises a fifth, then moves up a step to a minor sixth and falls back to the fifth was an established symbol of deepest despair. Bach has begun the subject with a variation of this melodic progression but instead of rising the fifth to F, he descends to it then leaps a minor ninth to G-flat (an interval, in itself, a symbol of distress) and falls back to F. The despair embodied in this theme is made even more real to us when we see that the first four notes form the cross motif.

The answer descends a fifth, an interval equally found to express agony in minor key melodies such as the opening chorus of Cantata 38 *Aus tiefer Not schrei' ich zu dir* (Out of deep despair I cry to thee). Note that this melody also moves to the fifth, minor sixth and back to the fifth.

With a theme of just six notes, a consummate expression of the soul begging not to be forsaken.

As is often the case where there are many voices and stretti, there is no regular countersubject, but the figure of four rising scale notes is so integral throughout, it may be considered as such. The juxtaposition of the calm, steadfast steps of this motif with the implied anguish of the subject is surely significant.

The bond between the Fugue and its Prelude is noticeable not only in the appearance of several passages in double thirds but also in the character of the development section that begins at bar 25. As in the Prelude at bar 13, an aura of quietude is felt as the soprano gently emerges from the D-flat major cadence. Within this section the rhythmic pattern ♪♪ ♩ in bars 42–44 echoes the pattern ♪♪ ♩ in bars 13–14 of the Prelude. But this period of reprieve evolves into a powerful climax when the soprano, in an agonized leap of a minor seventh, and in stretto with the alto, soars to the high C-flat—the same realm Bach took the soprano for the intense climax at bar 16 in the Prelude.

From the E-flat minor cadence the fifth episode prepares the way for the conclusion which reaches epic proportions when all the voices state the complete subject in a magnificent stretto maestrale. Who can fail to grasp the pathos of the descending fifth motif in the alto and tenor voices in the final moment of this deeply moving Fugue?

Prelude, B-Flat Minor, Book II

The four pieces in B-flat minor Bach wrote for the WTC can be seen as unified not only in mood but also as a complete unfolding of a particular emotional experience. Knowing the Prelude and Fugue in this key in the first book heightens our awareness of the affect of those in the second book.

This hauntingly beautiful Prelude is a continuation of the deep sorrow expressed in the earlier pieces but is of a soul-searching, reflective nature. We will see that it looks back to both the Prelude and the Fugue in the first book and also contains intimations of the emotional transformation that will become evident in its companion Fugue.

The first theme consists of 12 notes, a holy number in Bach's works, a symbolic reference to the Apostles, and by inference to faith. It begins with a descending four-note scale and then we hear the poignant interval of the falling fourth, both motifs elements of the subject of the Fugue in this key in Book I. Within the last six notes of the melody is a rising fourth, historically a fundamental religious symbol. It also appears in the inversion of the opening melody in bars 5–6 and 59–60, and is prominent in many other passages in the course of the music. A second theme follows, which is actually an extension of the first one, and together they form a complete musical sentence. We recognize it as the main theme of the B-flat minor Prelude in the first book and its presence may indicate the tempo of the piece. That Bach referred back to that Prelude and wanted its theme to be heard again, and to be an integral part of this Prelude, is a matter for deep contemplation as we study this piece. He has now placed it in a setting free of anguished dissonance. Its appearance in combination with the first theme forms a musical expression of exquisite tenderness and pathos.

The two themes are heard throughout the piece in the original sequence but not always in the same voice. Only once, in bars 25–27, does Bach put them directly in counterpoint. Yet the second theme is often accompanied by the descending scale motif of the first theme—a subtle ongoing communion between the two melodies.

The two themes appear for the last time well before the end of the piece, but notice that the alto, at the conclusion of the second theme, is given a very special melody in the approach to the B-flat minor cadence. It is, except for one note, the opening motif of the subject of the Fugue that follows.

Now begins the magnificent coda. The rhythmic and melodic patterns of eighth notes which have been flowing ceaselessly throughout the music, infusing a sublime aura around the themes, now forms a kind of apotheosis, a sense of divine mercy lifting the spirit from the burden of the sorrow. In the final moments, the melody which foretells the opening of the Fugue is clearly sung in the soprano just before the strong major cadence.

In this Prelude, Bach's inspiration and supreme contrapuntal mastery reaches transcendental levels.

Fugue, B-Flat Minor, Book II

We come now to a work which, by almost universal consensus, is the most powerful Fugue in the WTC and one of the greatest Bach ever wrote. Monumental both in contrapuntal skill and intellectual discipline.

It is a difficult Fugue, demanding the utmost in concentration, technical skill, and interpretive insight. Intimidating as this may sound, as always with Bach, even limited mastery brings its rewards. You will not fail to grasp and be affected by the spiritual force of the music.

Despite the intimation at the end of the Prelude of an easing of the burden of sorrow, the subject clearly indicates that the soul is still deeply troubled. In addition to the inherent character of the theme, Bach uses, without exception, the rarest and most dissonant forms of imitation—those at the seventh and the ninth.

Like the Fugue in B-flat minor in the first book, this theme begins with two notes followed by a rest. But what a difference in sound! Two hesitant but determined steps in half notes which, following the rest, evolve to more quickened quarter notes—the theme is now fully revealed after its foretelling in the Prelude. The melody that follows, now moving even more rapidly, comes directly from the undulating waves of eighth notes near the end of the Prelude. All these motivic figures are now transformed in character to create the imposing theme, a theme imbued with the strength of an indomitable will to overcome adversity and reaffirm faith. In the Prelude we saw the symbolic reference to the number 12—a symbol of faith. Here too, Bach has again represented this number. The subject is stated 12 times, and there are 12 episodes.

Bach faithfully adhered to the basic doctrine of the theory of affects— one piece, one mood. The musical language included rhythmic, melodic, and motivic formulas for expressing various affects.

Now let's look at the elements which make Bach's language so absolute in the affection of this Fugue. The opening six-note motif is definitive in three ways—the rhythm, the three stroke notes (marcato and detached) and the falling diminished fifth which Bach then repeats at the end of the subject. This melodic interval will have a far-reaching influence on the tenor of the Fugue, for it also occurs in its rising form in the inversion of the theme.

The ascending chromatic scale, which is the entire theme of the first countersubject, is a motif Bach often used to create intense emotional effect. One dramatic example is in the *St. Matthew Passion* where the Evangelist, in recitative no. 73 *Und siehe da, der Vorhang im Tempel*, describes the cataclysmic events following the crucifixion. The bass line ascends chromatically to depict the opening of the graves and the rising of the saints. (See Chapter 6, Prelude in D minor Book II, for the illustration of this passage.) Another example is found in chorus 23 of the *St. John Passion*. When Pilate asks what charge they bring against Jesus, the fanatical crowd erupts with the vehement words *Wäre dieser nicht ein Übeltäter* (If this man were not a malefactor), which Bach sets to a rising chromatic theme, dreadful and frightening in its effect.

In the second countersubject Bach adds three more stroke notes, harsh thrusts, continuously pitted against the flowing eighth-note melody of the subject. Two countersubjects equally as passionate and strong as the subject.

In the fifth episode (at bar 37) Bach introduces a new motif—the descending chromatic scale, historically a symbol of sorrow and grief. This is a beautiful moment in the Fugue, touching in its tenderness with each imitation of the motif cadencing on a major chord. With this episode, Bach leads to the entrance of the inversion of the subject and in counterpoint with it, the inversion of the first countersubject which now becomes the descending chromatic motif.

The subject undergoes a metamorphosis in its inversion. This melody has an aura of despondency, of darkness overshadowing the confidence and steadfastness. Bach develops these opposing themes independently and at great length—41 bars for the subject and 38 bars for the inversion.

At bar 80 the inevitable confrontation between the two emotional forces begins. In a series of stretti the themes rage in conflict, culminating, in the final stretto with each theme doubled in voices, in an epic climax. The appearance of double thirds in contrary motion at this intense moment is not without a deeper significance. For it was with this pattern that Bach created the torturous climax near the end of the Prelude in B-flat minor in the first book.

We have come on a remarkable journey through the key of B-flat minor in the WTC. The Prelude in the first book tells that an event causing deep sorrow has taken place. Its companion Fugue is filled with lamentation following this event. The Prelude in the second book is reflective, seeking to understand, and its companion Fugue is permeated with the resolve to surmount adversity.

Scholars tell us that the themes in this Fugue present a multitude of contrapuntal possibilities. Bach chose judiciously. The power of affect was the most important criterion, never just virtuosic display of skill.

This great Fugue is a supreme manifestation of the unfathomable depth of his genius.

23

B Major

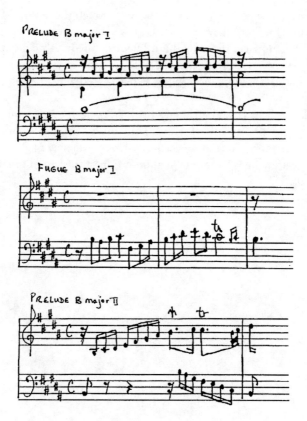

PRELUDE B major I

FUGUE B major I

PRELUDE B major II

In the Baroque period, E major was the "key of heaven," since it was the sharpest and therefore "highest" key then in common use. With the advent of mean-temperament tuning (equal-temperament came later), it became possible to compose music in keys of five, six, and seven sharps. This did not alter the attributes of E major but extended, as it were, the concept of a "heavenly realm" through even "higher" major tonalities. Bach's four pieces in the *WTC*, in which he introduced the key of B major to the literature, are supreme manifestations of this concept. All are masterpieces of elegance, charm, beauty of melodic and rhythmic design, and unsurpassed craftsmanship. A priceless gift, composed exclusively for those to whom he dedicated the *WTC*. Except for the Passepied II in the French Overture, he wrote no other compositions in this key.

Prelude, B Major, Book I

Bach begins the group in this challenging key with a piece which is relatively accessible. Making no difficult technical demands, he entices and inspires confidence. The design of the Prelude is a paragon of simplicity. The music revolves around one melodic motif.

As in the E major Prelude in Book I, Bach transports us again to a pastoral setting, as exquisite in mood and vision but graced with the vibrant colours of the B major tonality.

The rising melodic figures in the opening statement evoke an image of dawn and a sense of pending sunrise. The whole development from here on will take us through the gradual unfolding of this earthly miracle.

In the first section of the Prelude the main motif moves from voice to voice in a gentle dialogue, each imitation reflecting a gradual awakening to the new day. The modulation to F-sharp major marks a subtle change in the atmosphere, a sense of expectation heightened by the syncopated rhythm in the alto and a leap to a higher register in the soprano. This sense is intensified as the harmony moves to the key of G-sharp minor. This is a pivotal moment in the scenario. Bach depicts signs of increased excitement and emerging activity by introducing two elements in the melodic patterns. First he modifies the main theme with a rocking figure, a figure he features prominently in all the Preludes in keys of five, six and seven sharps devised of other melodic patterns, and then follows it with a melody that dances with a delightful rhythmic joy motif ♪♫♩♫♩, at the same time flying through G-sharp minor, C-sharp minor and E major.

At bar 15 we expect a cadence onto the tonic. But no, he raises the suspense, delaying this key, adding now an inversion of the theme and, with a stroke of the pen, assures us of the arrival of the long-awaited moment by adding a fourth voice, doubling the rising step motif, and combing the theme with its inversion. With the addition of a fifth voice in the final tonic chord, the Earth is bathed in the light of the risen sun.

Fugue, B Major, Book I

Compared to the flurry of excited activity so vividly depicted in the Fugue which followed the pastoral Prelude in E major, Bach has chosen a more temperate mood for this Fugue. An aura of serene happiness pervades the music, subjective in nature and contemplative in the surrounding beauty of the scene created in the Prelude.

The first thing I want to mention about the subject is that it consists of 14 notes. As has been noted throughout the book, this is the numerical symbol for Bach's name (2 + 1 + 3 + 8 = 14), which he encoded in a piece as a personal identification with or an intimation of his presence in the spirit of the music. The fact that he has encoded it here in the main theme, and thus at the very heart of the piece, adds a very special dimension to its affect.

Elements of the subject immediately form a direct link with the Prelude. It begins with the same three notes. This is followed by an ascending tonality, this time a scale with the rhythmic joy motif which appeared in the middle section of the Prelude. An expression of joy further illuminated with a trill.

The countersubject shares equal prominence with the subject. Full of character and individuality, it is the perfect complement. In its original form as presented in the exposition, it contains a leap of the sixth, an interval which, when Bach wrote it in a context such as this, is always an expression of joy. This theme also has an ascending tonality, a scale that appears in canon with that in the subject, but with its own rhythmic pattern. Of the two themes, this is the one which plays a pictorial role, creating an image of lively activity, the world rejoicing in the new day.

Who but Landowska (*Landowska on Music*) would detect the song of a bird in a little melodic motif heard in the countersubject during the third entry of the subject? It is the cuckoo. Can you find it? It is heard once more. But wait. Let's see what is happening with the countersubject. After the exposition it goes flitting from voice to voice, soprano to alto, bass to soprano, and in the process changing its melodic form to suit the occasion. It is during the fifth and redundant entry of the subject that it makes the first leap to freedom, so to speak, and it is here that we hear the second song of the cuckoo.

Between these two little bird song motifs, Bach completes the exposition and places the first episode. In it, and in the two other episodes as well, in addition to the rhythmic motif ♫♩ another melodic motif from the companion Prelude appears—the step-rising scale sung by the alto at the beginning and the step motif in double thirds which lead to the Prelude's cadence. In the third episode this motif in double sixths heightens the approach to the final section.

After the fifth entry of the subject, the second episode begins the move away from the tonic key, an ephemeral modulatory passage for the sixth to enter in F-sharp major. This entry foreshadows a transition in mood, for after it the subject suddenly appears in inversion. A feeling of melancholy surrounds this passage, as though thoughts on the transience of life's moments of happiness and contentment have crept into the contemplation. This mood continues even when the theme returns in its original form in bar 21, and is even more poignant in its next appearance during which the melody drops a diminished fifth as it modulates to C-sharp minor.

At this point the third episode begins, lifting the veil of melancholy with modulations through F-sharp minor, E major, to B major. When the ninth entry appears the joyful mood is again restored. With the tenth and last entry in the Comes (answer) and in the highest tonal level in the piece, with the countersubject finally returning in its original form, it is ecstatic.

In the penultimate bar a simple little melodic motif is heard in canon just before the final cadence, which Bach will later choose as the beginning notes of the beatific second subject of the Fugue in this key in Book II.

The beauty of its simplicity is the essence of the spirit of serene contentment in which this Fugue closes.

Prelude, B Major, Book II

In the two pieces in this key in the first book the ambient mood is one
of serene happiness amidst an earthly pastoral setting. In his Prelude for the
second book Bach lifts us to the fields of Elysium, realm of supreme and
everlasting joy. He does this with music exquisite in its transparency, beauty
of flowing melodies, and an aurora borealis of constantly shifting harmonic
colors.

One of the striking features worth noting as we begin the study of this
Prelude is the similarity in Bach's concept for its opening statement with
that of the next "highest" tonal key—F-sharp major. Both begin in an improvisatory style and then settle into a rocking broken-chord pattern. The material on which each is designed and developed is, however, very different. This
Prelude has the characteristics of a Toccata but without any of the bravura
and virtuosity associated with a true Toccata.

Bach begins the Prelude with a rising tonality just as he did in the two
pieces in this key in Book I. And no less symbolic in its intent. Here, as a
rising scale, it is direct and immediate. As it appears in some choral works,
it describes a literal "going forth"—as we see in the Gethsemane scene in
the *St. Matthew Passion*. But when it is combined with a descending scale,
as in this Prelude, we find another dimension. In the organ Chorale Prelude BWV 644 *Ach, wie nichtig, ach, wie flüchtig* (Ah, how empty, ah, how
fleeting) the reference is to the transience of earthly life and happiness.

We see this reference again in the alto recitative in Cantata BWV 64, *Geh,
Welt! behalte nur das Deine... Der Himmel ist nun meine* (Begone, world! just
keep your possessions ... Heaven now is mine). A solo cello plays an ascending scale six times, a descending scale three times, then a final seventh

ascending as she sings of the transience of worldly attachments and the
glory of heavenly joy. In this case the figure intimates an awakening, a going
forth to a higher consciousness. An intimation underlying the affect of this
Prelude.

The piece is divided into six sections, each having distinct characteristics. Waves of ascending and descending scale patterns prepare the transition
from one to the next. Each new section seemingly appears as a spontaneous
new thought in an improvisatory process.

In three of these sections Bach brings forward, as a continuing thread,
three motifs from the previous pieces. The first is heard near the end of the
first section at bar 9, the melodic motif in the soprano which looks both
back and forward. It appeared at the end of the Fugue in Book I and, as
mentioned there, will form the beginning notes of the second subject of the
coming Fugue. It will appear again near the end of the Prelude in bar 42.

The second motif, appearing in the second section, is the rising step
motif which was sung by the alto at the beginning of the Prelude in Book
One, and carried forward to the episodes in its companion Fugue. Here,
Bach transforms it into a rising chromatic melody, its effect creating dramatic tension within a thickening of the texture by the addition of a third
voice, and foreshadowing a modulation to G-sharp minor. During this modulation, in bars 15–16, we hear again the motif which looks toward the coming Fugue, now extended and forming much more of the melody that will
form the second subject.

The third motif appears in the fourth section, a beautiful little dance
interlude. After three bars of a jaunty melody with appoggiatura ornaments
(played ♪. ♪., although sometimes dubiously played as a ♫♫ pattern),
in bar 26 the rhythmic joy motif ♫♩ appears, as delightful here as it was
in the Prelude in Book I, and made all the more charming by the graceful
sigh motif figures (notated by Bach) that follow it.

The fifth section intimates a transition from the elation of the dance
interlude to a mood of expectation. A sublime sequential melodic pattern
moves through descending harmony after which a series of broken chord
patterns gradually build a feeling of suspense, reaching palpable intensity

in the diminished chord with its throbbing heartbeat pedal-bass, until finally pausing at the F-sharp cadence.

A rising scale in the bass heralds not only the return of the opening theme. It is the awaited moment of revelation. The signature tonic scale is first joined by its counterpart, then soars in the soprano in a blaze of glory. After this ecstatic climax a sense of deep and abiding joy permeates the music as it descends in waves of scale and chord patterns and comes to rest on the final chord. A breathless silence follows this chord, as if something more wondrous is still to come. Indeed, there is.

Fugue, B Major, Book II

The progression from the Prelude to the Fugue marks the ultimate stage in this spiritual journey through the B major tonality. From a pastoral ambience to the fields of Elysium, Bach now lifts us to an empyreal realm. Thematic beauty, rhythmic symmetry, harmonic and technical mastery—all are inimitable in this sublime double Fugue.

The serene character of the first subject sets the tone immediately. Its long sustained note values indicate that the piece is in a vocal style, with legato predominant. Two features of this theme hold considerable significance. The melody rises in tonality as in the three other pieces, and in particular, spans a tonic octave as did the opening scale theme of its companion Prelude. In addition, the entries of the subject in the exposition appear in ascending order from bass to soprano. The other, vital to the affect of the work, is the symbolism associated with the length of this theme. It consists of seven notes, that most holy of numbers, sacred since antiquity. A symbol of the Holy Spirit, the miracle of creation, and the gateway between Earth and heaven.

Last but not least, yet another numerical symbol is connected with this theme. In the Fugue in this key in Book I there are 14 notes in the subject. As noted then, this is the symbol for Bach's name. In this Fugue there are 14 entries of the subject. An affirmation of a continuing personal bond with the spirit pervading throughout the pieces in this key.

The countersubject, with its own rising tonality and rhythmic pattern ♫ ♩, which is a variation of the rhythmic joy motif ♫♩ heard in all the other B major pieces, contributes to the uplifting spirit of the subject. Incorporated in this melody is the interval of the fourth, another religious symbol, sacred since the time of Pythagoras. It is formed between the half notes emphasized by accented off-beats and the ascending tonal progression of each rhythmic joy motif, and will be pronounced in important sections of the piece. The syncopated motive of this countersubject will appear several times during the development.

There is a second countersubject in the exposition. It is heard in the bass in the third and fourth entries at bars 11–12 and 15–16 and also has a rising tonality. Note, too, that the last two notes of this melodic motif form the interval of the fourth. After the exposition, the complete six notes of the second countersubject will be heard only once more—its third appearance occurring with the third entry of the second subject in bars 33–34. Yet it will continue to echo throughout the Fugue for its four inner notes form the essence of the melody of the second subject.

The first episode now appears as a prelude to the entry of the second subject. In it Bach brings forward three melodic motifs from the Prelude in Book I. The first, sung in the alto in bar 22 and repeated in the bass, is the lovely rocking motif heard in bar 12 in the Prelude. It has also been called a "peace" motif. Two bars later the alto sings the original form of this motif as heard in bars 9 and 10 in the Prelude.

Both these motifs are preceded by a short descending scale motif, seemingly insignificant, but it is, in fact, featured in all three preceding pieces. It will later be a major factor in one of most exalted passages in the development. The third is the rising step motif sung in the tenor in bar 23, which was the alto melody at the beginning of the Prelude. You will, I'm sure, immediately sense the implication of this motivic connection with the first piece in the set.

The cadence of the episode in F-sharp marks the entry of the second subject, a melodic theme which will add an extraordinary dimension to the affect. Among Bach's pictorial figures, a melody that ascends and descends in a regular flowing pattern is often characteristic of a "flight of angels" symbol. Its identification is based on the Chorale Prelude *Vom Himmel kam der Engel Schar* BWV 607 (From heaven came a group of angels), and the first of the canonic variations on the chorale *Vom Himmel hoch, da komm' ich her* BWV 606 (From high heaven come I here), as well as several Cantata numbers. The character of this melody clearly suggests just such an interpretation of this second subject. With the inclusion of this pictorial image the spiritual ambience is fully manifest. The meaning of the descending motion of the melody is evident. Its appearance is not confined to the first subject but is woven through the episodes as well. After its entry, the angelic presence is constant through to the end.

The entry of this theme could not be more clearly announced and continues aurally distinct during the exposition. The order of the tonal positions of the entries are not without significance. Soprano in mid-high range, bass in mid-low range, soprano in high range and finally, bass in low range. Ingeniously, Bach creates an aura of a surrounding celestial presence.

A short episode leads to the development where the combining of the two melodies is not only a masterful display of craftsmanship but also a profound meditation on their symbolic relationship. In the first part of the development modulations through minor keys continually shift the tonal colors, but all are leading to the golden entry in E major, the "key of heaven," when once more we hear the "angels" theme ring out in its highest register.

Bach follows this entry with the fourth episode, a passage abounding in numerical symbolism and one of the great moments in the Fugue. Underlying the apparent serenity of the first five bars is a subtle intimation of growing emotional intensity which suddenly erupts in a fervent outpouring in the next three bars. It is in this passage that the number 3, one of the holiest since the time of Pythagoras, symbolizing wisdom, peace and justice and, in biblical terms, the Trinity, is combined with the number 4, the sacred symbol of God. It is scored for three voices. In a rising tonal sequence three proclamations of the interval of the fourth in the soprano are repeated in canon by the alto and tenor. Each soprano proclamation is accompanied by the scale motif, its rapid descending motion accentuating the upward thrust of the melodic fourth. Completing the powerful imagery evoked in this episode is yet another numerical symbol. It is twelve bars long and after its cadence the first subject makes its 12th entry—specific by the absence of the second subject. The number 12 is a symbol of faith and trust.

For the approach to the last double entry Bach has given the sixth episode a rich harmonic texture with sequences of parallel thirds, an interval from the time of Pythagoras right up to the Middle Ages considered a detested dissonance but "in the Renaissance became an incarnation of sensuous bliss" (Mellers, *Bach and the Dance of God*, p. 40).

Translated by Bach to a more elevated level, it defines the state of ecstasy in which the first subject makes its 14th and final entry, at its highest tonal pitch in the Fugue, and in E major—the "key of heaven." The inclusion in the coda of the "peace" motif is particularly affecting, as is the "angel" theme heard alone just before the Fugue closes. In keeping with its numerical entry, the 11th, a number with dark innuendos, its melodic formation in a diminished harmony has a tinge of nostalgia—like a gentle farewell. But how affirmative the cadence is with the clear resounding rising fourth in the soprano, which the tenor, after a long silence, firmly reiterates.

24

B Minor

Unlike Mozart, who approached B minor with great caution, Bach composed an abundance of compositions in this key. It is the quantity as well as the exceptional quality which has led to the belief that B minor was indeed his favorite key. It inspired him to monumental heights in the choral and vocal solo genre and the creation of magnificent instrumental pieces.

The instrumental works include Invention no. 15, Sinfonia no. 15, Partita for solo violin BWV 1002, Sonata for violin and clavier BWV 1014, Sonata for flute and clavier BWV 1030, organ Prelude and Fugue (the Great) BWV 544, and the Orchestral Overture BWV 1067.

Among the choral works the following are prime examples: the *Kyrie* in the *B minor Mass*; in the *St. Matthew Passion*, the Aria e Coro which begins the second part, the soprano solo *Blute nur, du liebes Herz!* (Bleed now, thou dear heart!), and the alto solo *Erbarme dich, mein Gott!* (Have mercy, my God!); and the alto solo *Es ist vollbracht* (It is fulfilled) in the *St. John Passion*. Two other arias express a different sentiment from the Passions but are significant to the key: in Cantata BWV 79, the aria (duetto) *Gott, ach Gott, verlass die Deinen nimmermehr!* (God, ah God, leave Thy people nevermore); and in the secular Cantata BWV 215, the soprano aria *Durch die von Eifer entflammten Waffen* (Through weapons inflamed by zeal) in which the theme of repaying evil with kindness is the hero's (August III) way.

In the Prelude and Fugue in the first book, the mood is associated with the spiritual intensity of the Mass and the pain and suffering in the Passions. In the second book, it is more closely attuned to the spirit of the last two arias quoted. But, as we will see, Bach makes subtle connections between the two sets.

Prelude, B Minor, Book I

Pathos and sorrow lie at the heart of this Prelude, deeply moving in its meditative character and the expressive power of its musical language. It is the awareness of different elements of this language which influences our approach to style of interpretation, and our emotional response to the music.

Bach's indication of a tempo is significant since he rarely did so in the

WTC. Andante in his time was not a slow tempo but rather one which flows with ease yet constant momentum. The pizzicato bass establishes the pace, builds the harmonic structure, and augments the affect of the melodic figures of the duo above it with an unrelenting throbbing rhythm.

The melodic formation of the four-note theme contains two revealing symbolic elements. It begins with a rising interval of the fourth—a fundamental religious number, sacred as a reference to God since antiquity, and the melody forms a cross symbol which can be seen if a line is drawn from the first note to the third and another between the second and fourth. This theme signifies a deep relationship between the Prelude and the *B minor Mass*, where the first of many appearances is in the opening number, the Kyrie (Lord, have mercy on us).

Another instance where Bach used this theme in a context of pain and sorrow is in the Duo e Coro *So ist mein Jesus nun gefangen* (So is my Jesus now taken) in the *St. Matthew Passion*. It is heard in the beautiful introductory section, played by flute and oboe and accompanied by a pizzicato continuo.

The first section of this binary Prelude is devoted to imprinting the affect inherent in the theme. The canonic treatment of this melody brings into focus another dimension of the affect. This is the tension created by the dissonance of constantly occurring suspensions on intervals of the second, and suspensions resolving on chords of the seventh.

Even though the theme of sorrow is clearly stated in the opening bars, Bach immediately makes a highly significant modulation to D major, a most positive key, signifying inner strength and confidence. It is not only singularly ornamented with a melodic flourish of 16th notes, but it occurs at the 7th bar, the holiest of numerical symbols.

As the first section approaches the cadence before the second part begins, the bass, beginning with the last note of bar 15, and for the first time, sings the theme. A signal that it will now become a major factor in the dramatic emotional development which will unfold. Immediately as the second part begins it sings in canon with the duo above it, then accentuates its participation with three great leaps. A short passage then follows which is, as it were, the calm before the storm. Note particularly the gentle melody in the soprano in bar 24—it will be an important motif in the coming Fugue, and emit the same benign aura amidst turmoil and pain.

The modulation to F-sharp minor marks a turning point from a meditation on sorrow to an impassioned outpouring of anguish. This transition begins with the alto significantly altering the theme by rising a tritone (diminished fifth), a most disturbing interval known as the *Diabolus in musica*, symbolizing darkness and evil. The soprano follows with an equally painful leap of a minor ninth on to a diminished seventh chord. Once again the alto begins the theme with the tritone, after which the tension briefly subsides as the harmony eases its way down from D major to cadence on a G major chord. But the anguish cannot be repressed. In a succession of ascending melodic patterns the soprano builds the tension to a painful climax, culminated with a diminished third, an interval associated with acute anguish, and one that Bach used rarely and only at critical moments.

The descent from this climax does not fulfill the expectation of release. At bar 42, instead of a closing tonic cadence, a deceptive cadence begins a coda which, in effect, prolongs the grief. Leaps of diminished fourths and fifths in the alto and soprano and chromatic scale figures in the bass fill the passage with dissonance. Of further significance in this passage are the series of descending chromatic seconds, all of which anticipate the sigh motifs in the subject of the companion Fugue.

Yet after this bitter climax, Bach closes the Prelude with two poignant phrases and a tierce de Picardie. A symbolic affirmation of faith and confidence.

Fugue, B Minor, Book I

When we consider that when Bach completed this set of pieces he had, as far as we know, no plans to compose a second set, we gain a perspective of the serious contemplation which must have preceded his ultimate plan for the final piece. That this final statement should be on the theme of suffering does not reflect a morbid preoccupation. It was this universal experience and its meaning which deeply concerned him all his life.

He was only 37 years old when the set was completed in 1722. But he knew intimately the pain of loss and hardship: The death of both his parents before he was 10 years old, of three children during his marriage to Maria Barbara and most devastating of all, her sudden death in 1720.

This, his last piece in the set, in a key of deeply symbolic associations, and the longest in duration in the whole *WTC*, is a profound meditation on the theme and its affect in musical language of almost painful clarity.

As he did for the Prelude, Bach has again indicated a specific tempo. In his time, largo meant slower than adagio and also carried a sense of solemnity. This term influences our approach to the music in realizing the full effect and implications of the harmonic chromaticism and measured pulse of rhythmic patterns.

The subject is extraordinary in melodic design and symbolism. It consists of 21 notes, a multiple of three and seven, two most sacred numbers, symbols of the Trinity and the Creator, respectively, and indicative of the spiritual frame on which the affect is built. There are three sets of melodic figures which form a cross symbol when a line is drawn from the first to the fourth notes and from the second to the third. These three figures are composed of the descending chromatic seconds heard at the end of the Prelude, now marked with slurs by Bach—sigh motifs, symbols of weeping. The tritone (*Diabolus in musica*) occurs between notes 7 and 8, and two accented leaps of the diminished seventh, an interval associated with pain, are heard in the second and third figures. Finally, unprecedented, and pivotal for the affect, the theme contains all 12 notes of the octave—especially noted, as you would expect, by Schoenberg.

The countersubject, in its initial appearance, augments the affect of the subject with an unresolved tritone and diminished fourth. Deliberate dissonance is created at decisive points of juxtaposition with the subject. This is maintained throughout its relationship with the subject. Most notably though, it is the final phrase of this melody which affirms the Fugue's affinity with the Kyrie (Lord, have mercy on us) in the *B minor Mass*.

Even though it goes through continuous transmutation and cross-voicing, the countersubject always ends with this Kyrie melodic motif during the trill in the subject.

This phrase with the Kyrie motif is immediately echoed in the first episode between the second and third entries and repeats it twice in the second episode leading to the fourth entry. As the piece unfolds, we become very aware of the importance of this supplication amidst the depiction of sorrow and pain.

With the third episode Bach begins the development, and here he brings forward the melodic figure from bar 24 in the Prelude. He now reveals the intrinsic beauty of this motif by its diatonic contrast to the chromaticism, which by its very nature creates a spiritual dimension inherent in Bach himself. This is the consciousness of a compassionate spiritual presence in times of great distress.

The undulant character of the melody suggests it may be a "flight of angels" symbol and, indeed, the harmonic modulations through A major and D major reflect this symbolic image. He will relate this melodic passage to the number 3, the symbol of the Trinity. It will appear only three times. The modulation to F-sharp minor with its melancholic association is a poignant moment. The alto begins to sing the theme but after only three notes stops, as though overcome with grief. Only after another bar of the "angelic" music is it able to begin again and complete the theme. In episode four Bach re-creates the emotional scenario more intensely. When the tenor too sings only three notes of the theme and cannot continue, the soprano leaps a dramatic octave raising the sonority of the celestial music, as if to emphasize the certitude of divine presence. Like the alto, the tenor now can complete the theme.

As in the preceding episodes, this next one also begins with the Kyrie motif. There is no angelic music now. The themes of suffering and supplication dominate the episode, as does the number 5, a symbol of pain (the number of wounds inflicted on Jesus on the cross). Not only is it the fifth episode, its length is five bars. But Bach has woven into the design the number 3, symbol of the Trinity. Two incomplete statements of the theme consisting of only the first nine notes (3 × 3) are sung in stretto by the alto and soprano. The episode ends with three supplicant Kyrie motifs. This is followed by the seventh (numerically significant) entry of the theme, sung by the bass as though in response to the faltering attempts by the alto and soprano.

In episode six, the number 3 is once again present. It is three bars long and has three stretti of the nine-note fragment of the theme. The dominance of this symbol in this passage leading to the eighth entry has a direct bearing on the tonality of this entry. It begins in D major and involves all four voices. This strong key brings into focus an emerging cosmic dimension to the theme. This is strengthened by the ninth entry, which also begins in D major, and again is marked by being in four voices. To stress the significance of the voicing of these D major entries, of the 76 bars of this Fugue only a total of 17 are in four voices. This dimension is heightened in the following episode. It is the seventh and as the numerical symbol of the Creator, the seven appearances of the weeping Kyrie motif in it has powerful implications.

The 10th entry plays a vital role in the approach to the climactic end of the middle section. Without resolving on a cadence, it joins with the other voices in a modulation specific for this moment in the Fugue. For Bach is preparing the 11th entry, one with deep symbolic implications. St. Augustine attributed to the number 11 *Transgressionem decalogi notat* (10 + 1 Trespass of the holy commandments)—the sinner. It is also believed that redemption is implicit in Augustine's attribution. Of utmost importance is the key Bach chose for this entry. It is E major, the "key of heaven" (the sharpest key then in common use, thus the "highest"). It is emphasized descriptively by an E major ascending scale in the alto in the preceding bar and in the alto accompanying the bass entry. The union of the symbolism of the number 11 and that of the key has, I suspect, very personal overtones, and is the soul of the affect of the Fugue.

This is immediately reflected in the next entry of the subject, the 12th, a number symbolic of faith. Bach has lifted the tonality entirely to the treble, and follows it with the eighth episode in which the long-awaited beatific melodic passage makes its third and last appearance.

The emotional intensity of this passage elicits an impassioned entry of the subject in the tenor with the alto doubling the sigh motifs, and the countersubject soaring in the soprano. But something extraordinary happens. The theme breaks off after the ninth note and passes to the bass. By closing the tenor theme on E and D-sharp Bach has prepared for the final statement of the complete subject to be not only the 13th but in the key of E minor, the Passion key. He has raised the theme of pain and suffering and redemption to the realm of the cosmos—magnificently climaxed with three Kyrie motifs of the countersubject above rhythmically and tonally penetrating ascending chromatic chords.

Bach returns from the realm of E minor to B minor to state the theme as he began—in the alto. It does not need to be complete. Just the nine note segment, extended in the soprano with a melodically acute diminished third (a special link with the companion Prelude) and a final Kyrie motif in the bass, dynamically emphasized with a leap of a major seventh, embody the essence of everything that has come before. Trust in divine purpose behind all pain and sorrow is affirmed in the glorious cadence.

Prelude, B Minor, Book II

Bach returns to the theme of suffering and sorrow for his first piece in the B minor set for the second book. Now in his fifties and nearing the end of his life, he approaches the theme in a mood of contemplation, his thoughts and feelings expressed in transcendent musical language.

His appointment in Leipzig was fraught with dissension, irrational, often petty, criticism, and thwarts to almost every innovation to raise the standard of excellence.

We do not know exactly when he began the second book, but the completion is dated 1744. What we do know is that he compiled the set during a time of crisis which dates from 1730 to 1743. It was a time when he increasingly distanced himself from opposing factions and sought refuge in composing works which meant a great deal to him on a personal level.

There are two versions of this Prelude. The first, marked allegro, has an alla breve time signature and moves in eighth notes. The second, changed by Altnikol, and likely approved by Bach, has a 4/4 time signature, moves in 16ths, and omits the allegro (an important detail—the tempo is moderate and fluent). In citing bars the first number refers to the Altnikol version, the number in the original version in parentheses.

The Prelude is divided into seven sections, the sacred numerical symbolism in the design forming the foundation on which the affect will develop.

The first section is the exposition of the main melodic theme. Suffering and sorrow lie deep within the haunting beauty of this opening passage. The melody contains five broken chord melodic figures each of which forms the cross symbol. A fusion of numerical and visual symbols of pain. The four turns are an ornamented form of the interval of the diminished third, a symbol of anguish. Over the bass statement of the theme Bach introduces a descending melodic motif, particularly plaintive in the second pattern with its drop of a minor seventh. And to end, the last notes of the soprano are a weeping sigh motif, specifically annotated with a slur by Bach.

In the B minor Fugue in Book I, faith and trust evolve through pain and sorrow. It is reflected now in the second section which begins in bar 5

(9). To prepare this section the bass makes a dramatic leap down a major seventh. A definitive association of this interval with faith and certainty is found in the great soprano aria *Mein gläubiges Herze* (My believing heart) in Cantata BWV 68. She sings, "Away lamentation, away mourning...my Jesus is near." With these last words the melody ends with a drop of a major seventh.

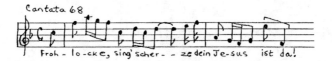

This interval is heard three times, the numerical symbol of the Trinity. Combined with this, though, is syncopation within a new melodic phrase in the upper melody—a rhythm often denoting uncertainty and doubt in the choral works. Note the alternating direction of the turns in conjunction with this rhythm. This conflict intensifies as the harmony ascends to the key of D major, a most positive key, where the third section begins at bar 9 (17).

In this section Bach again introduces a new motif above the bass statement of the theme. This motif, with its questioning leaps, also appears three times. Again there is a combination of certitude in D major with uncertainty in the motif. This results in a darkening of the harmony to E minor, the Passion key. As the bass sings the theme we hear the weeping sigh motif sung three times in the soprano (annotated with slurs by Bach) which culminate in another questioning leap, then plunges headlong into the theme to begin the fourth section.

With this E minor statement of the theme the bass sings the plaintive descending motif from the exposition. After singing the theme the soprano suddenly leaps a 10th to sing a new phrase which begins with a mournful fall of a 4th in bar 17 (33)—so reminiscent of the beginning of the B-flat minor Fugue in Book I and the F-sharp minor Prelude in Book II. Beneath it the bass sings the melody introduced in section two, its syncopated melodies augmenting the poignancy of the soprano's lament. The sequential repetition raises the emotional intensity to a climactic anguished outburst, palpably depicted in a series of torturous tritones, then finally subsides to the melancholy mood of F-sharp minor, which dominates the fifth section.

Reflecting the numerical symbol, Bach gives this section solely to the main theme and, although only a partial statement in each voice, by refiguring the beginning of the theme in the bass, the cross symbol figure appears five times.

The sixth section reveals the soul still tormented with uncertainty and doubt. A series of syncopated rising broken chords of the minor seventh, then a rising diminished seventh with its tritone closely followed by another tritone, depicts the soul passing through a crisis which pauses on a melodic figure rising a minor sixth and falling back to the fifth—a symbol of deepest despair.

Bach now begins the seventh and final section of the Prelude with the seventh full statement of the theme and, as in the third section, combined with the questioning motif. Still seeking an answer, the soul makes one last plea. Now in the tonality of B minor, the motif, begun with a falling fourth, heightened by three anguished diminished thirds ornamented as a trill (shared with the theme), and increasingly higher leaps, builds to an impassioned climax on two *five-voiced* chords. Despite the assurance intimated by the rising scale and accented drop of the major seventh, the subsequent descending scale and cadence on the minor five-voiced chord closes the Prelude in a spirit of resignation.

Fugue, B Minor, Book II

Often, the first impression of this Fugue is that it is jovial and even whimsical. But Bach chose the passepied dance form not to denote a gay and carefree mood, but one both serious and profound. It is the vigorous rhythmic pulse of this form which was vital to the affect he planned for the piece. That he would end the B minor group with a work which seemingly has no connection to the sentiment expressed in the other three pieces is inconceivable. Indeed, he has incorporated something from all the preceding pieces in this key into the design of the Fugue, each reference of considerable significance in the realization of the affect.

The opening five-note melody of the subject is one that Bach used to begin the B minor duet *Verzage nicht, O Häuflein klein* (Despair not, O little flock) in Cantata BWV 42. It is a message of encouragement to the faithful not to despair against the enemy.

But also in this opening melody is the first reference to the preceding pieces. The first three notes are the same as those of the subject in the Fugue in Book I. In addition, the subject is the same length—21 notes, the multiple of 3 and 7, the two sacred numerical symbols of the Trinity and the Creator, respectively. The outstanding feature of the theme is, of course, the octave motif. If we look back to the companion Prelude we can see in the leaping octaves in sections two and six an anticipation of their appearance in the Fugue. A clue to the symbolic meaning of this figure can be found in the aria (duetto) *Gott, ach Gott, verlass die Deinen nimmermehr!* (God, ah God, leave Thy people nevermore!) in Cantata BWV 79, where it has been described as a "tumult" motif.

The association is both a plea for strength in the midst of adversity and a confidence in eventual triumph. It is the spirit of this interpretation which can be readily identified in the subject, and thus the affect on which the Fugue is based.

The first countersubject echoes the opening melodic figure of the subject before moving into a melody dominated by a trill. The dynamic dimension this trill passage adds to the exposition of the subject intensifies the feeling of turmoil. Once brought into this stage of the scenario it remains a dominant force, even in the episodes. But its role is confined solely to the exposition. Bach then replaces it with a second countersubject—for which some of us are grateful.

The second countersubject now enters and will stay steadfast with the subject to the end. With its melodic emphasis on dissonant leaps of the seventh, it is, in effect, another form of a tumult motif. The force of the impact of the octave motif in the subject is strengthened by the rapid leaps of the countersubject, leaving no doubts about the gravity and sincerity of the supplication, reflected in the key of F-sharp minor.

A response comes immediately in the episode where the beatific melody heard in both the Prelude and Fugue in the first book appears in the alto, and the harmony modulates to D major.

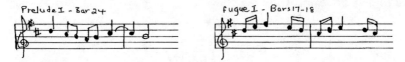

The theme, its sentiment imbued with the positive overtones of D major, rings out in the highest tonal pitch in the Fugue. The aura of grace surrounding this passage is enhanced in the following episode where the beatific melody leads the modulation to A major—a Trinity key, in which the theme enters, resonant in the lowest tonal pitch.

Yet doubt and uncertainty still lie deep within. Bach depicts this conflict in phrases of ascending chromatic harmony in which a series of *Diabolus in musica* tritones are imbedded. An extraordinary detail of this passage must not be missed. All 12 tones of the octave occur—a defining feature of the Fugue in Book I. The ensuing lapse into the melancholy of F-sharp minor is characteristic after such a depiction. The episode evolving from the mood of the theme in this key combines commiseration through sequential descending scales with an unmistakable symbolic spiritual presence in the series of rising intervals of the fourth.

A unique stretto of the initial motif of the theme marks the beginning of the last section of the Fugue. This stretto underscores the penultimate entry of the subject and its special tonal realm. In direct relationship to the pathos of the preceding passages, it is in E minor, the Passion key.

Bach follows this with a sublime episode where the octave motifs in the bass and open intervals of the fourth in the alto illuminate the transcendent soprano melody.

The stage is set for the ninth and final entry of the subject. Reflecting the numerical symbolism of its position (a multiple of three, the Trinity), the episode following this strong statement is radiant with the celestial melodic motif in stretto.

A reiteration of the ascending chromatic phrases evokes two fervent *Verzage nicht* (Despair not) exhortations. A rising and descending scale, which was heard at the end of the companion Prelude, is, as then, integral to the cadence.

As does the *St. Matthew Passion*, this great Fugue closes with an appoggiatura on the final chord. In contrast to the *Passion*, here the dissonance resolves affirmatively. Pain, turmoil, and doubt are at rest at last.

Bibliography

Altschuler, Eric Lewin. *Bachanalia: The Essential Listener's Guide to Bach's Well-Tempered Clavier.* Boston: Little, Brown, 1994.

Bach, Carl Phillip Emanuel. *Essay on the True Art of Playing Keyboard Instruments.* Trans. W. J. Mitchell. New York and London: Norton, 1949.

Badura-Skoda, Paul. *Interpreting Bach at the Keyboard.* Oxford: Clarendon, 1995.

Bettmann, Otto L. *Johann Sebastian Bach: As His World Knew Him.* Secaucas, N.J.: Carol, 1995.

Bodky, Erwin. *The Interpretation of Bach's Keyboard Works.* Cambridge, Mass.: Harvard University Press, 1960.

Bruhn, Siglind. *J. S. Bach's Well-Tempered Clavier: In-depth Analysis and Interpretation.* 4 vols. Hong Kong: Mainer Intl., 1995.

Casals, Pablo, and Albert E. Kahn. *Joys and Sorrows: Reflections by Pablo Casals, as Told to Albert Kahn.* London: Macdonald, 1970.

Collins, Ernest S. *Elements of Eroticism in the Church Cantatas of Johann Sebastian Bach.* West Vancouver, B.C.: n.p., 1985.

Craft, Robert. *Stravinsky: Chronicle of a Friendship, 1948–1971.* New York: Knopf, 1972.

David, H.T., and A. Mendel. *The Bach Reader.* New York: Norton, 1966.

Franklin, Don O., ed. *Bach Studies.* Cambridge: Cambridge University Press, 1989.

Furlong, William Barry. *Season with Solti: A Year in the Life of the Chicago Symphony.* New York: Macmillan, 1974.

Geiringer, Karl. *Johann Sebastian Bach: The Culmination of an Era.* New York and London: Oxford, 1966.

_____. *Symbolism in the Music of Bach.* Washington, D.C.: Library of Congress, 1956.

Goldberg, Laurette. *The Well-Tempered Clavier of J. S. Bach: A Handbook for Teachers and Performers.* Berkeley, Calif.: MusicSources, 1995.

Gray, Cecil. *The Forty-Eight Preludes and Fugues of Johann Sebastian Bach.* Oxford: Oxford University Press, 1938; DaCapo Reprint Series, 1979.

Grew, Eva Mary, and Sydney Grew. *Bach.* New York: Collier, 1966.

Herz, Gerhard. *Essays on J. S. Bach.* Ann Arbor, Mich.: UMI Research, 1985.

Hindemith, Paul. *Heritage and Obligation: J. S. Bach.* Westport, Conn.: Greenwood, 1950.

James, Jamie. *The Music of the Spheres: Music, Science and the Natural Order of the Universe.* New York: Copernicus, 1995.

207

Keller, Hermann. Trans. L. Gerdine. *The Well-Tempered Clavier by Johann Sebastian Bach.* London: Allen & Unwin, 1976.

Kupferberg, Herbert. *Basically Bach.* New York: McGraw-Hill, 1986.

Landowska, Wanda. *Landowska on Music.* Ed. and trans. D. Restout. New York: Stein and Day, 1964.

Ledbetter, David. *Bach's Well-Tempered Clavier: The 48 Preludes and Fugues.* New Haven, Conn.: Yale University Press, 2002.

MacPherson, Stewart. *Das Wohltemperirte Klavier: A Commentary on Book I.* London: Novello, 1934.

Marshall, Robert. *The Music of Johann Sebastian Bach: The Sources, the Style, the Significance.* New York: Schirmer, 1989.

Mellers, Wilfrid. *Bach and the Dance of God.* London: Faber & Faber, 1980.

Payne, May de Forest. *Melodic Index to the Works of Johann Sebastian Bach.* New York: Peters, 1962.

Quantz, Johann Joachim. *On Playing the Flute.* Trans. Edward R. Reilly. New York: Free Press, 1975.

Riemann, H. *Analysis of J. S. Bach's Wohltemperirte Clavier.* London: Augener, 1921.

Rosen, Charles. *Bach and Handel.* Chapter in *Keyboard Music*, ed. Denis Matthews. New York: Pelican, 1972.

Rothschild, Fritz. *A Handbook to the Performance of the 48 Preludes and Fugues of J. S. Bach According to the Rules of the Old Tradition.* London: Adam & Charles Black, 1955.

Scherchen, Hermann. *The Nature of Music.* London: Dennis Dobson, 1946.

Schrade, Leo. *Bach: The Conflict between the Sacred and the Secular.* New York: DaCapo, 1973.

Schweitzer, Albert. *J. S. Bach.* 2 vols. Trans. Ernest Newman. London: Black, 1952.

Spitta, Philipp. *J. S. Bach.* 2 vols. New York: Dover, 1952.

Stravinsky, Igor, and Robert Craft. *Expositions and Developments.* London and New York: Faber & Faber, 1962.

Tatlow, Ruth. *Bach and the Riddle of the Number Alphabet.* Cambridge: Cambridge University Press, 1991.

Terkel, Studs. *The Spectator.* New York: New Press, 1999.

Tovey, Donald Francis. *Bach: 48 Preludes and Fugues, Books I and II.* London: Oxford University Press, 1924.

Universal Bach: The Lectures Celebrating the Tercentenary of Bach's Birthday. Philadelphia: American Philosophical Society, 1985.

Valenti, Fernando. *Performers Guide to the Keyboard Partitas of J. S. Bach.* New Haven, Conn.: Yale, 1990.

Wolff, Christoph. *Bach: Essays on His Life and Music.* Cambridge, Mass.: Harvard University Press, 1991.

_____. *Johann Sebastian Bach: The Learned Musician.* New York: Norton, 2000.

_____, ed. *The World of the Bach Cantatas.* New York: Norton, 1997.

Young, W. Murray. *The Cantatas of J. S. Bach: An Analytical Guide.* Jefferson, N.C.: McFarland, 1989.

Index